M000296230

PHP Code Performance Explained

printed on October 30, 2018

This book will guide you through **the challenges of managing the performance** of your applications. During our journey, you will learn more about topics like profiling techniques or performance testing, but more importantly, you will learn how to integrate performance supervision into your day-to-day development workflow.

PHP Code Performance Explained

ISBN-13: 978-2-918390-36-7

Blackfire
92-98, boulevard Victor Hugo
92 115 Clichy
France

This work is licensed under the "Attribution-Share Alike 3.0 Unported" license (*http://creativecommons.org/licenses/by-sa/3.0/*).

You are free **to share** (to copy, distribute and transmit the work), and **to remix** (to adapt the work) under the following conditions:

- **Attribution**: You must attribute the work in the manner specified by the author or licensor (but not in any way that suggests that they endorse you or your use of the work).

- **Share Alike**: If you alter, transform, or build upon this work, you may distribute the resulting work only under the same, similar or a compatible license. For any reuse or distribution, you must make clear to others the license terms of this work.

The information in this book is distributed on an "as is" basis, without warranty. Although every precaution has been taken in the preparation of this work, neither the author(s) nor Blackfire shall have any liability to any person or entity with respect to any loss or damage caused or alleged to be caused directly or indirectly by the information contained in this work.

If you find typos or errors, feel free to report them at support@blackfire.io. This book is continuously updated based on user feedback.

Contents at a Glance

Chapter 1

Introduction

10 years ago, writing unit tests for a project was not a widespread practice in the PHP world. As a matter of fact, PHPUnit only reached *version 1.0*[1] in mid-2004. How did we know our projects were bug-free back then? By clicking around, literally. After fixing a bug, or adding a new feature, developers would browse their applications like crazy to check that nothing was broken. Needless to say, this was a tedious, boring, and error-prone process. After a while, developers and project managers were doing less manual testing and bugs were "unintentionally" deployed to production servers and regressions were common. In a way, customers and end-users were in charge of the quality assurance.

Nowadays, everyone writes unit and/or functional tests for their PHP applications. At least, everyone should as we now have great tools like PHPUnit, Behat, Codeception, Selenium, and more. If you are not writing tests, you probably feel bad about it, right?

People don't write tests because it's fun or easy. We write tests because the **cost of a bug** or a regression is gigantic. A bad user experience has a direct, negative impact on **business reputation** and damages a company's **bottom line**. This is nothing new. According to Boehm and Basili's "Software Defect Reduction Top List" published in 2001, the cost of fixing a bug is **15 times more expensive** after release (from $937 in development to $14,102 in production).

What about performance? How many developers continuously test the performance of their applications? According to my own experience, not that many. What's more, nobody feels ashamed for not writing performance tests; probably because the existing tools are not good enough. Unfortunately, performance issues have the same impact as bugs: **bad user experience leading to less engagement and revenue loss**.

How do you ensure that the performance of your applications is good enough **before** going to production? Are you using a load-testing tool? Are you benchmarking your code? How do you find bottlenecks?

---

1. https://sebastian-bergmann.de/archives/300-PHPUnit-1.0.0-Released.html

We've all used the simple `microtime()` PHP built-in function for testing performance. I've used it myself for many years to try to optimize my PHP projects. It is frustrating to say the least. `microtime()` can only tell you part of the story: some code takes more time than it should. This is okay, but it cannot tell you why the code is slow or how you can improve it. Even if you find a bottleneck, validating a fix is difficult as numbers can vary widely from one run to the next, and the seemingly innocuous changes can have negative impacts on other parts of the code.

The point is that it is easy to make stupid performance mistakes: n + 1 queries when using an ORM is the first one that comes to mind, but they are many other ones.

The *n + 1 query* problem occurs when getting children records of a main record with an ORM. When lazy-loading is enabled, the ORM will get the main record from the database and then issue n additional queries for the children records; the more children you have, the more queries are issued, and the slower the code becomes.

Performance management is not something you do once, just before you release your code. In order to be effective, performance management must be included in your day-to-day workflow via deep integrations into your development stack. That is what I'm going to write about in this series.

Good tools go a long way. Some solutions have been around for many years, but thanks to Blackfire, many more people are now optimizing their projects dramatically:

- *trivago: Continuous Performance Monitoring for PHP - The tale of Blackfire at trivago*[2]: " Blackfire allowed us to: Enforce a backend performance budget to stop continuous performance degradation over time; Detect performance bottlenecks before they're deployed to production; Offer a common platform for PHP developers to discuss performance related issues. "
- *Improving Symfony VarDumper by 30%*[3]
- *Creatuity: Improving RuralKing's Magento shop*[4]: SQL time was improved by up to 72% on a critical page of RuralKing's checkout!
- *How we sped up Sylius' Behat suite with Blackfire*[5]: The Sylius test suite is now 6 times faster and consumes 90% less memory!
- *Optimizing league/commonmark with Blackfire.io*[6]: Two simple changes led to a whopping 52.5% performance boost!

In the next 23 chapters, I will guide you through Blackfire's features and discuss how you can leverage Blackfire to better test your application's performance

---

2. https://tech.trivago.com/2017/10/27/continuous-performance-monitoring-for-php---the-tale-of-blackfire-at-trivago/
3. https://github.com/symfony/symfony/pull/23683/
4. https://blog.blackfire.io/creatuity-magento-performance-refactoring.html/
5. http://lakion.com/blog/how-did-we-speed-up-sylius-behat-suite-with-blackfire
6. https://www.colinodell.com/blog/201511/optimizing-leaguecommonmark-blackfireio

in an automated and continuous way. You will also learn that Blackfire is not just about performance; it is also a great tool to help you achieve **better code quality**, **improved security** and **best practices enforcement**.

But first, why is performance so important? *According to Google*[7]: **53% of visits are abandoned if a mobile site takes longer than 3 seconds to load**. Your customer is gone, probably forever. If your web applications are not fast enough, you will lose both customers and revenue. That's why performance optimization is key to success. Ready to learn more?

---

7. https://www.thinkwithgoogle.com/data-gallery/detail/mobile-site-abandonment-three-second-load/

Chapter 2

Performance as a Feature

Nobody would ever intentionally deploy a broken application. If your unit tests are failing, that's a big red flag. However, people deploy applications that are much slower than their current version every single day. Performance is not seen as a feature. Requirement specifications go into great detail about end-user features, design, user experience, etc, but these documents rarely mention the need for speed.

If your website is broken because of a bug, all developers are going to work around the clock to fix it as fast as possible. Performance issues should be receiving the same level of attention, but sadly that's not yet the case. I think this is because we lack good tools. **You cannot fix something that you are not aware of**.

However, managing performance is not just about magic tools. **Performance management is about culture and processes**. But why should you care so much about performance?

Performance impacts your Business

Big companies and well-known startups demonstrate over and over again that there is a direct correlation between the time it takes for an application to respond and your levels of user engagement, conversions, and ultimately revenue.

Two examples:

1. *Aliexpress*[1] reduced load time by 36% and saw a 10.5% increase in orders and a 27% increase in conversion for new customers.

---

1. https://edge.akamai.com/ec/us/highlights/keynote-speakers.jsp#edge2016futureofcommercemodal

2. *Pinterest*[2] rebuilt their pages for performance led to a 40 percent decrease in wait time, a 15 percent increase in SEO traffic and a 15 percent increase in conversion rate to signup.

It's even worse for mobile applications. Optimizing APIs and *UI performance*[3] is critical for modern mobile applications.

Need some more examples? Here are some conclusions from major players:

- *Google: 2% slower = 2% less searching per user*[4]
- *Yahoo! 400 milliseconds faster = 9% more traffic*[5]
- *AOL: Faster pages = more page views*[6]
- *Shopzilla: 5 seconds faster = 25% more page views, 7 to 12% more revenue*[7]

Still not convinced? Try your site on *Google's Speed Scorecard*[8]. Better, if you're working on an eCommerce site, it can also calculate the revenue impact if you change your site's speed. You'll soon figure out how fast you can get your return on investment for working on performance!

People don't like to wait when browsing the web or navigating through a mobile app. 3 seconds of wait is what the average person tolerates nowadays, and that number is going down every day. Google's recommendation is actually to keep the server response time below 200ms (time it takes to load the necessary HTML to begin rendering the page from your server, subtracting out the network latency between Google and your server).

Adoption of @blackfireio is improving the technical performance, and hence the commercial performance, of our website.
— Sam Burns (@AgileTillIDie) September 25, 2015

Measuring Performance

What makes our applications slow? What kinds of tools can we use to improve performance?

Modern cloud platforms sell us infinite resources, which sounds great... but this is a false promise if you don't also have an infinite budget to match. Most of us have limited resources at our disposal: CPU time, network, disks, memory, etc. **Improving performance is all about optimizing resource usage.**

---

2. https://medium.com/@Pinterest_Engineering/driving-user-growth-with-performance-improvements-cfc50dafadd7
3. https://www.smashingmagazine.com/2015/10/rail-user-centric-model-performance/
4. https://assets.en.oreilly.com/1/event/29/Keynote%20Presentation%202.pdf
5. https://www.slideshare.net/stoyan/dont-make-me-wait-or-building-highperformance-web-applications
6. https://assets.en.oreilly.com/1/event/29/The%20Secret%20Weapons%20of%20the%20AOL%20Optimization%20Team%20Presentation.pdf
7. https://conferences.oreilly.com/velocity/velocity2009/public/schedule/detail/7709
8. https://www.thinkwithgoogle.com/feature/mobile/

At a macro level, performance depends on a large number of factors including the time it takes to:

- Generate the page's content on the server (the backend);
- Transmit the data from the server to the client;
- Display the page in the browser (the frontend).

On modern web applications, the lion's share of the time is spent on the application server and the browser.

Major browsers provide good built-in tools that help you understand how pages are rendered and *JavaScript executions*[9].

On the server, most of the time is spent executing the application code you wrote, which usually includes calls to third-party services like a database server, a cache system, some external web services, and more. To better understand **code behavior at runtime**, the **code needs to be instrumented**. Code instrumentation generates useful data for identifying slow code and figuring out how to fix it.

Profiling Tools

Measuring and analyzing the performance of an application is the charge of **profiling tools**. A profiler instruments the code you want to measure and generates data about its runtime behavior. It does so by **instrumenting** the code. Data collected during this process could include:

- The memory consumption;
- The number of times functions are called;
- The duration of functions' execution;
- The number of SQL queries;
- ... and much more.

Be warned that code instrumentation adds some overhead to the runtime execution. As such, it impacts time measurements. In other words, measuring time takes time! This is why good profiling tools must have minimal (or at least constant) overhead to avoid skewing results too much. Keep that in mind when choosing your tool.

Automation

Using a profiler for ad-hoc analysis is great, but managing performance over time requires that you continuously check your code's behavior and get immediate feedback to avoid regressions. The best strategy is to manage performance on a day-to-day basis during development and testing, but also on your staging and production servers. Integrating a profiling technology like Blackfire into your

---

9. https://developers.google.com/web/tools/chrome-devtools/profile/rendering-tools/js-execution?hl=en

continuous integration/deployment workflow is key to success and one of the main selling points of Blackfire.

Conclusion

As you might have guessed by now, Blackfire is a profiler, but it is also so much more. In the next chapter, I will compare Blackfire to other performance-related solutions to give you a better understanding of what makes Blackfire unique.

Chapter 3

What is Blackfire?

Blackfire is a **performance management solution**. The core technology is a **profiler**, but the product is way more than that. Blackfire fits in your **development workflow** by providing the following key features:

- A low-overhead profiler that helps developers **debug** performance issues, **find** hidden bottlenecks in existing codebases, and **validate** the impact of fixes. In production, the profiler helps **diagnose production issues**, understand problems, and find solutions fast.
- A platform that stores data history to allow **trend analysis** over time and **collaboration** within larger teams.
- Key Integrations with testing libraries, automation software, and **continuous integration** and deployment platforms to **automate performance testing**, give **fast feedback** to developers, **avoid regressions**, and **guarantee** that applications can be deployed with confidence.

Although Blackfire is a unique, integrated performance solution **for the complete application development lifecycle**, there are other solutions available that attempt to solve a subset of these problems. In some cases, these solutions can be used as a complement to Blackfire.

Blackfire vs microtime

microtime() is a built-in PHP function and probably the simplest way to determine how long a snippet of code takes to execute:

Listing 3-1

```
1   $start = microtime(true);
2
3   // do something
4
5   $stop = microtime(true);
6   error_log($stop - start);
```

Using microtime() may be easy, but this approach suffers many drawbacks. First, you must instrument your code manually. How do you know where to start? Which piece of code do you profile first? It's like shooting in the dark. What's more, when you end a microtime() "profiling session", you will have to go through your code and remove the code you added. And if you want to run a profile again in the future, you will need to start from scratch.

Using microtime() for profiling is like using var_export() or echo to debug a script when you'd be better off using a tool like Xdebug. Blackfire automatically instruments your code from inside PHP; there is no code to add to your project.

Another problem with the microtime() approach to profiling is that it only tells you part of the story; the time it takes for a piece of code to execute tells you nothing about how you can improve your application's performance.

Perhaps the most significant problem with the simple microtime() approach is that it assumes your code executes at the same speed every time and that a single profile is a reliable measurement of performance. Taking only one measure is not enough, you need several iterations:

Listing 3-2

```
1   $start = microtime(true);
2
3   for ($i = 0; $i < 10; $i++) {
4       // do something
5   }
6
7   $stop = microtime(true);
8   error_log(($stop - start) / 10000);
```

In addition to this average time, you should also calculate the **standard deviation**. If it is too big, reasoning about the numbers becomes very hard and often just plain wrong.

Blackfire takes several measurements of the code execution and aggregates them to get more accurate results. More importantly, time comes in several flavors. Besides the wall-clock time (what microtime() returns), Blackfire also gives you the CPU time and the I/O time of each function call; we will cover this topic in a few chapters but you can imagine that understanding if your code is I/O bound or CPU bound makes finding the root cause of a performance problem much easier.

But Blackfire cannot perform miracles and it suffers from the same core problems when it comes to measuring time; that's why Blackfire also provides **other dimensions that do not depend on time** and are more stable (like memory usage, and more specific metrics like the number of executed SQL queries, web service calls, and more - we will cover those metrics in great depth in this series).

Blackfire vs Benchmarking Libraries

There are many well-established PHP benchmarking libraries available today. These tools offer a nice alternative to microtime() and avoid most of the repetitive, boilerplate code from above, and often include calls to `memory_get_usage()` to provide information about memory consumption. Developers can use these tools to determine which implementation of a given algorithm is faster.

Benchmarking tools are compelling as they are written in PHP and don't require a complicated installation. But like pure `microtime()`, they lack many features needed to seriously manage performance of large codebases.

When using a benchmarking library, choose one that calculates the standard deviation and checks that the difference between two algorithm implementations is **statistically significant**.

Blackfire vs Xhprof

Xhprof is one of the oldest pure-profilers in the PHP world. Open sourced by Facebook in 2009, it provides a low-overhead profiler that you can use on development machines. Some libraries built on top of Xhprof can also be used in production, where they will take profiles on a certain percentage of incoming requests.

Xhprof is provided as a source package, and it's up to you to compile and install the library, which can be difficult. Furthermore, Xhprof is no longer maintained by Facebook and the future of the library is uncertain. Several forks have been created, but as of this writing, support for PHP 7 is still not available.

Blackfire started as a fork of Xhprof, but after some time we decided to start over from scratch to give ourselves more flexibility, lower the overhead significantly, and still provide more features.

One of the main differences is that Blackfire automatically instruments source code without any code changes. Not only does it ease the process, it also allows Blackfire to gather more information about the runtime execution (destructors behavior for instance or insights about PHP garbage collector behavior).

Blackfire is supported, packaged, and maintained for many different platforms and configuration management tools.

Xhprof provides a minimal web interface with large tables of numbers and static image call-graphs that are hard to navigate and most of the time impossible to generate for larger applications.

Blackfire comes with a modern and fast web interface that lets developers navigate profiles and call graphs, and works with large codebases.

Being a SaaS product, storage and profile life-cycles are automatically managed by Blackfire. Also, Blackfire adds a security layer on top of the profiler to make it conveninent and secure to profile projects on production servers and let large teams collaborate on performance.

Xhprof only provides a profiling tool, and as such, it does not come with any permanent storage nor management tool for profiles.

Last, but not least, Blackfire does not add any overhead when it is not running a profile. This is very important for production servers, where Blackfire only instruments the code when a profile is triggered by an authorized user.

Blackfire vs New Relic

New Relic is an Application Performance Management (APM) solution. It monitors mobile and web applications in real-time, enabling developers to diagnose and fix application performance problems. New Relic supports many languages, including PHP, and offers some additional features like a server monitoring service.

New Relic essentially monitors real-user interactions with a website. It collects data for each request, like the time it takes PHP to generate a response, SQL queries, HTTP calls, but also some information about browser-side rendering.

For some requests (key transactions), New Relic gathers more data and provides a small call graph. As it monitors real-user requests, the instrumentation must have the smallest overhead possible and the profiling data it provides is less comprehensive than what full-featured profilers like Blackfire can provide.

Blackfire does not monitor web applications. Its core technology is rooted in the profiler world. Blackfire never instruments real-user requests. Instead, authorized users are responsible for triggering Blackfire manually when a performance issue is detected. Blackfire can also be run automatically on a pre-defined schedule, or in response to specific events like when a new version is deployed to production.

Blackfire is useful throughout the application development lifecycle, not just in production. Using Blackfire, developers can continuously measure and improve application performance. The best an APM like New Relic can do is alert you when your production site is slow, which is much too late. By integrating Blackfire into your development workflow you are helping developers understand why their code is slowing down earlier in their process, before these issues reach production.

Blackfire gives developers the right information at the right moment.

A unique Blackfire feature is its comparison mode. This helpful call graph view gives you a visual representation of the impact of your changes and makes it much easier to validate that a bottleneck has been resolved.

Moreover, modern web stacks rarely consist of just an HTTP endpoint. Most projects run command-line tools on the server on a regular basis, like consumers or daemons. Blackfire provides the same set of tools to manage their performance like the ones available for HTTP requests.

New Relic is a great complement to Blackfire. Whenever it finds a slow page, run a Blackfire profile to analyze and resolve detected problems.

Blackfire vs Load-Testing Solutions

There are many load-testing solutions available on the market, from Open-Source solutions to hosted server farms able to simulate thousands of simultaneous users.

Load-testing helps to determine a system's behavior under both normal and peak load conditions. It helps to identify the maximum number of simultaneous users an application can accept without too much service degradation. As load-testing operates at a macro level, hitting an application's entire infrastructure, it does not give you any information about why you hit a limit and why you cannot serve more requests per second.

Load-testing solutions are a good complement to Blackfire. You can trigger some Blackfire profiles on some key HTTP requests while a load-test is in process to better understand how your code behaves under stress. These profiles might give you some nice insights about bottlenecks that would be difficult to spot under normal circumstances.

Blackfire vs JMeter

JMeter is an Open-Source software application designed to load-test functional behavior and measure performance. It simulates a browser by running pre-defined user scenarios. Like load-testing solutions, it operates at the infrastructure level.

Scenarios are defined in the JMeter interface, which is very powerful and allows for great report customization. JMeter supports many protocols, not just HTTP.

Blackfire offers a similar scenario feature, which lets you simulate complex user interactions. These scenario reports contain profiles for all executed HTTP requests and give you detailed insights into what exactly is going on in your application: the number of SQL queries executed, number of emails sent synchronously, number of compiled templates, cache usages, ...

One big difference between JMeter and Blackfire is that Blackfire doesn't load-test the application when running the scenarios like JMeter. It is however possible to combine JMeter and Blackfire by configuring JMeter to automatically trigger Blackfire on some requests and generate a nice report about code behavior under stress.

Blackfire vs Google Chrome

Google Chrome and other browsers offer nice built-in profiling tools. Their goals are similar to Blackfire's but they operate on the **client-side code** (JavaScript, DOM rendering, ...) whereas Blackfire operates on the **server-side code** (PHP).

You should use such tools alongside Blackfire to be able to optimize the end-to-end performance of your applications as experienced by real users.

Conclusion

Comparing Blackfire with other solutions is a nice way to better understand its features, but now it's time to test Blackfire on a project and see how it works.

During the next few chapters, we are going to use Blackfire to optimize a demo application and become more familiar with the main concepts of Blackfire.

Chapter 4
Your First Profile

Time to get our hands dirty! In this chapter, we are going to profile a real application and use Blackfire's web interface to understand its behavior and find some code optimizations.

The project we are going to work on is an Open-Source PHP project, *GitList*[1]:

> GitList is an elegant and modern web interface for interacting with multiple git repositories.

According to the Git repository, GitList "allows you to browse repositories using your favorite browser, viewing files under different revisions, commit history, diffs. It also generates RSS feeds for each repository, allowing you to stay up-to-date with the latest changes anytime, anywhere. GitList was written in PHP, on top of the Silex microframework and powered by the Twig template engine."

For the purpose of this tutorial, we have installed GitList on a demo server at *https://gitlist.demo.blackfire.io/* and set up a repository for Twig there. Blackfire has also been installed and configured.

Our goal is to find bottlenecks in the GitList source code and, if we find any, propose changes to optimize its performance.

Step 1: Gathering Data

The first step in our quest is to **gather data about the behavior of the current codebase** by using the Blackfire profiler. To do that, we will generate profiles for GitList's home page (/) and each of the tabs on the repository page: "Files" (/Twig), "Commits" /Twig/commits, "Stats" (/Twig/stats), and "Network" (/Twig/network).

---

1. https://github.com/klaussilveira/gitlist

Before we do this, you will need to *create an account on Blackfire.io*[2] if you don't have one yet. It takes less than a minute if you already have a GitHub or Google+ account.

Then, make sure to *start the free Premium trial*[3]. The basic Hack subscription doesn't enable to profile non-local HTTP applications. Premium does enable it, and also offers more profiling dimensions (such as SQL) and a lot more features you'll want to use in this tutorial, like assertions.

Next, be sure you have the Blackfire browser extension installed (Chrome and Firefox supported). We will use this extension to trigger our GitList profiles:

> The full instructions are available at *https://blackfire.io/docs/integrations/chrome* and *https://blackfire.io/docs/integrations/firefox*.

We are now ready to start our first profiling session!

To profile the GitList homepage, go to *https://gitlist.demo.blackfire.io/* and trigger a profile by clicking on the Blackfire Extension icon:

By clicking the profile button, you have asked Blackfire to begin profiling the page currently displayed in the browser. You should see a black toolbar at the top of the browser window with a nice progress bar:

 If anything does not work as described in this tutorial, do not hesitate to contact us.

---

2. https://blackfire.io/signup
3. https://blackfire.io/pricing

As you can see, it takes way more time to profile the page than it took to display it initially. This is because Blackfire triggers several page reloads behind the scenes to get a larger sample size, aggregate the results, and present more accurate information. Relying on only a single profile is not ideal, as we discussed in the previous chapter.

At the end of the profiling process, the toolbar displays a summary of the profile:

This summary provides some basic information (your numbers may vary slightly, but should be similar), from left to right:

- *26.7 ms*: the time it took for PHP to generate the GitList homepage;
- *4.69 ms*: the I/O time;
- *22 ms*: the CPU time;
- *1.15 MB*: the amount of memory consumed by PHP.

For now, we are only going to focus on main time and memory. We will discuss I/O and CPU in later chapters.

Front-end vs Back-end Profiling

Blackfire only profiles the PHP code executed on the server side or back-end. It does not profile the front-end (JavaScript execution, DOM rendering, ...).

Hooray! You've just generated your first profile.

Security: Profiling Authorization

Isn't that a major security issue? This would be a concern any other time, but we have specially configured the security on this server to allow anyone to run a profile, for the purpose of this tutorial. Rest assured, this would never be the case on your own servers. Blackfire's authentication and authorization mechanism is out of the scope of this chapter, but we will cover it later on in this series.

It took almost 27 ms for the server to generate the HTTP response. Is this good? Can we do better? When analyzing the performance of a project for the very first time, the slowest requests are the ones to optimize first. Now that we have our first profile, the baseline, let's profile another page and see if its performance is different from the homepage.

Let's profile the Twig project homepage, *https://gitlist.demo.blackfire.io/Twig/*. Load this page in your browser and use the browser extension to trigger a profile.

These numbers are quite different compared to the homepage. This page took more than *100ms* to render (vs *14ms*), and consumed around *2MB* of memory (vs *1.5MB*). It looks like this page can be optimized!

Step 2: Analyzing Profiles

The Blackfire summary toolbar is a good way to find which pages need to be optimized first, but then we need to dive deeper to better understand what's going on. Click on the "View Call Graph" button now. You should be redirected to the detailed profile on Blackfire.io.

Your profile should be similar to this one:

> *The profile is available at https://goo.gl/Tx1rTJ.*

Now it's time to learn how to use the Blackfire interface to detect performance issues.

The table on the left side of the screen displays a list of the main functions and methods that were executed. Clicking on a function name reveals the **resources consumed by this function**, like time, memory, network, ...

By default, **the most time-consuming function calls are listed first**. These functions are almost always where you want to look first. In our case, stream_select() comes first. It takes a significant amount of time to execute: almost half of the total time for 80 calls. As stream_select() is a PHP built-in function, it cannot be optimized; but we can try to lower the number of times it is called.

The next step is to understand which parts of userland code trigger these calls. Click on the stream_select() link to reveal this function's details, then click on the magnifying glass. The call graph will now be redrawn and centered on this specific node:

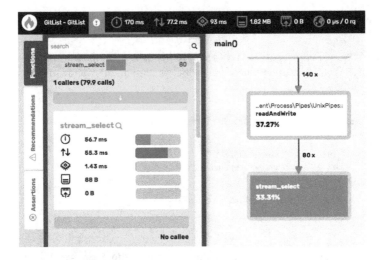

The **call graph** displays the executed code as a visual diagram where each **node** corresponds to a function or method call. The **edges** of the graph show the execution flow.

Now that we are focused on the stream_select() node, drag the graph up with your mouse until you find the Gitter\Client::getVersion() and Gitter\ Client::run() nodes. These are the first calls defined in userland PHP and the ones which we are most interested in:

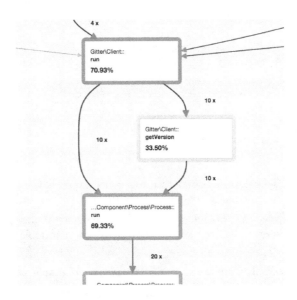

Step 3: Optimizing the Code

The `Gitter\Client::getVersion()` method is called *10 times* and accounts for *33% of the total execution time*, that's a lot. Its implementation reads as follows:

Listing 4-1

```
1   public function getVersion()
2   {
3       $process = new Process($this->getPath() . ' --version');
4       $process->run();
5
6       if (!$process->isSuccessful()) {
7           throw new \RuntimeException($process->getErrorOutput());
8       }
9
10      $version = substr($process->getOutput(), 12);
11      return trim($version);
12  }
```

Apparently, `getVersion()` returns the version of the local **git** CLI tool, as `getPath()` returns the path to the **git** binary. We can safely assume that this method will always return the same result for any given request (and most of the time even across requests).

Caching the returned value locally avoids running 10 identical sub-processes:

Listing 4-2

```
1   public function getVersion()
2   {
3       static $version;
4
5       if (null !== $version) {
6           return trim($version);
7       }
8
9       $process = new Process($this->getPath() . ' --version');
10      $process->run();
11
12      if (!$process->isSuccessful()) {
13          throw new \RuntimeException($process->getErrorOutput());
14      }
15
16      $version = substr($process->getOutput(), 12);
17      return trim($version);
18  }
```

And that's it. In less than 5 minutes, in a codebase we knew nothing about before, we've already found a performance bottleneck and written a patch.

Blackfire provided us the tools necessary to understand the code's actual behavior and showed us front and center exactly where to look to improve its performance.

We call that the "Blackfire effect", and *lots of people are experiencing*[4] it on their projects:

---

4. https://twitter.com/blackfireio/likes

Woot! Thanks to @blackfireio, @michaelthieulin and I optimized one of the backoffice pages of @dayuse_fr. The page was taking 18 seconds to load due to a misconfiguration of our @MongoDB indexes on a 15M documents collection. Now, the pages loads within 200 ms. pic.twitter.com/KmX4yYxTd6
— Hugo Hamon (@hhamon) July 3, 2018

Used @blackfireio seriously for the first time yesterday. Went from 1min 39s to 2.98s on some heavy data processing code... It transformed our workflow in amazing ways. Thanks!
— belisar (@belisar) March 24, 2018

I think I found a way to improve performance by 15% in @phpunit using @blackfireio. Our unit tests take 17 seconds normally and with the changes it shaves off a few seconds. When running a code coverage report with xdebug on it shaves off several minutes. I will submit a PR soon.
— Jonathan H. Wage (@jwage) February 13, 2018

Optimizing colinodell/json5 with @blackfireiohttps://t.co/nwFI5d9AHN #php #performance
— ?? Colin O'Dell (@colinodell) January 14, 2018

With #Symfony 3.4/4.0, enabling param 'container.dumper.inline_class_loader' can boost your dev env perf by 50% and your prod by +2%. For free as usual :) /cc @blackfireio pic.twitter.com/vvPoZlTZEb
— Nicolas Grekas (@nicolasgrekas) November 10, 2017

Reduced core page load by a further 30% today using @blackfireio timelines view. Killer feature in a killer tool
— Peter Ward (@petewardreiss) November 8, 2017

Conclusion

This is great, but we're not done yet. The complete process of performance optimization includes checking the impact of your code changes. First by running the unit tests to confirm that nothing is broken. Then, always compare the data between the current version of the code and the patched version to validate that the fix actually solves the problem and doesn't introduce regressions in other parts of the code.

Performance comparisons are a key feature of Blackfire; one that we will look at in depth in the next chapter.

Chapter 5

Validating Performance Optimizations

In the previous chapter, we learned how to profile an HTTP request directly from a browser. We learned how to find bottlenecks and how to read a call graph to find the code consuming most of the resources. We then wrote a patch hoping that it would improve the situation.

Now we need to validate that the fix has a positive and significant enough impact on performance. To do this, we are going to use **profile comparisons**, a unique Blackfire feature.

Step 4: Comparing Profiles (Code Changes)

We, as humans, are very bad at understanding how a computer works and how code is executed. It is impossible to know which implementation of an algorithm is going to be the fastest without a deep understanding of operating systems and your programming language implementation. Moreover, a patch improving one part of the code could potentially have a negative impact on another part of the application, making the overall speed actually worse.

Instead of guessing, we need hard numbers. Take a profile using the browser extension again on *https://fix1-ijtxpsladv67o.eu.platform.sh/Twig*, where we applied the patch from the previous chapter:

Listing 5-1

```
1   diff --git a/lib/Gitter/Client.php b/lib/Gitter/Client.php
2   index c806c1a..97a7aef 100644
3   --- a/lib/Gitter/Client.php
4   +++ b/lib/Gitter/Client.php
5   @@ -79,6 +79,12 @@ class Client
6
7       public function getVersion()
8       {
9   +       static $version;
```

```
10  +
11  +          if (null !== $version) {
12  +              return trim($version);
13  +          }
14  +
15             $process = new Process($this->getPath() . ' --version');
16             $process->run();
```

Without the patch, the profile summary looked like this:

And here is the new one with the patch:

The wall time went down from *118ms* to *82.6ms*, which was expected: the call graph tells us that even if `Gitter\Client::getVersion()` is still called 10 times, it only calls `Process::run()` once, which means that our cache works well:

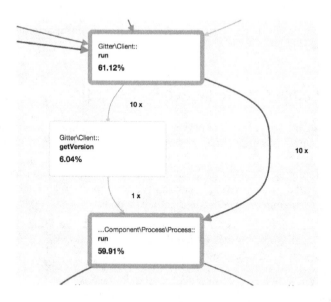

Running the GitList test suite shows that we didn't break any functionality.

We have just done a "manual comparison": we compared numbers and we looked for expected changes in the call graph. But there is a better way with Blackfire: profiles comparison.

Click on the Blackfire logo to view your Blackfire "Dashboard" (or go to https://blackfire.io when connected):

Click first on the "Compare" button on the second listed profile (the `Twig` profile without the patch) and then click on "Compare" again on the first listed profile (the `Twig` profile after applying the patch). Blackfire now *displays the comparison of the two profiles*[1]. The web interface looks very similar to the profile one but the call graph is now a visual representation of the comparison: faster nodes in blue, slower nodes in red:

> *The profile is available at https://goo.gl/4Ifyir.*

The summary indicates that there is a 30% time improvement between the two profiles, with our four-line patch, which is not too bad. Having a look at the numbers on the left and the colors on the comparison graph, we can conclude that there is no performance regression elsewhere:

---

1. `https://blackfire.io/profiles/compare/cb98e08e-91ee-41b6-b859-f2f2460e4ccb/graph`

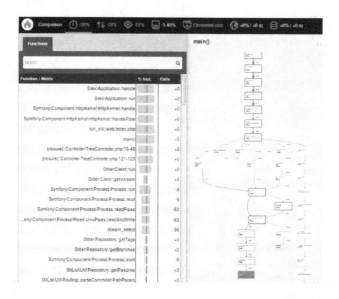

Step 2 (alternative): Comparing Profiles (Different Pages)

In the previous chapter, we used the homepage and the project page profile summaries to select the page we should optimize first. Then we looked at a profile of the project page to find optimizations.

Instead of doing this manually, we could have used the Blackfire's comparison feature to highlight performance differences:

> The profile is available at https://goo.gl/M4bZSF.

Not surprisingly, the comparison shows that the biggest slow down comes from the stream_select() call.

 You can also compare two random profiles, but if they are too many differences in the code, the results will not be useful nor easy to understand. Doing comparisons on requests using the same PHP libraries and/or the same framework gives better results.

Profiling Other Dimensions

Blackfire provides detailed data on many dimensions: wall time, CPU time, I/O time, memory, and network. Focusing on the wall time only, like we did on GitList, is just a first step.

A function consuming a lot of memory or getting a lot of data from the network has a direct impact on performance as well. The wall time already includes the impact of memory consumption or the impact of the amount of data retrieved from the network... but depending on the machine specifications or the network topology, the impact may vary widely.

Data retrieved over a network is an excellent example. On your local development machine, all project components are probably installed locally, so loading big payloads probably won't have a significant impact on performance as latency is very low in this situation. On production servers, where data can be hosted on a different server or even on a different network, latency and network speed can have a much bigger impact on the overall performance of your application. That's one of the reasons why you should optimize all dimensions, not just the wall time.

Always check all dimensions when looking for performance issues.

Profiling Again

30% improvement on the GitList project page is impressive, but can we do better? Profiling is a never-ending process. Whenever you fix a bug or add a new feature, you need to check the performance impact of that change.

Take 10 minutes now to look at the *project page profile*[2] again and try to find some more function calls that could be optimized.

Done? Did you find something? I did!

10 calls to `Gitter\Client::run()` still represents 60% of the wall time. Optimizing a function call can be done in two ways: optimizing some of the functions called by this method or reducing the number of calls to this method.

Use the search field on the left to find the `Gitter\Client::run()` call then click on the function name to reveal the detailed panel:

---

2. https://blackfire.io/profiles/32d9f72a-ed30-4e62-84b6-16185c0b9b57/graph

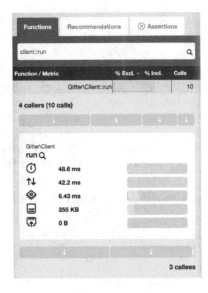

Besides the main dimension numbers, we learn that this method has "10 callers" and calls "3 callees".

A **callee** is a function called by our method, a child node in the call graph. Click on each callee arrow to review them all:

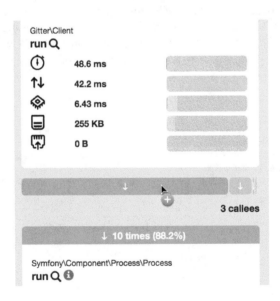

The two main callees come from the Symfony Process component, which we probably cannot optimize.

What about the callers? A **caller** is a function that called our method, a parent node in the call graph. Again, click on each caller:

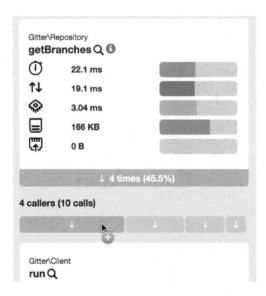

Are you thinking what I'm thinking? Gitter\Repository::getBranches() calls run() 4 times and Gitter\Repository::getTags() 3 times. The branches and the tags of a repository do not change that fast! I would even say that having different values within the same request could lead to hard-to-find bugs.

Using the same caching technique as before should help:

Listing 5-2

```
1  diff --git a/lib/Gitter/Repository.php b/lib/Gitter/Repository.php
2  index 42836f9..cd0aeba 100644
3  --- a/lib/Gitter/Repository.php
4  +++ b/lib/Gitter/Repository.php
5  @@ -233,12 +233,18 @@ class Repository
6        */
7       public function getBranches()
8       {
9  +        static $cache = array();
10 +
11 +        if (array_key_exists($this->path, $cache)) {
12 +            return $cache[$this->path];
13 +        }
14 +
15           $branches = $this->getClient()->run($this, "branch");
16           $branches = explode("\n", $branches);
17           $branches = array_filter(preg_replace('/[\*\s]/', '', $branches));
18
19           if (empty($branches)) {
20 -             return $branches;
21 +             return $cache[$this->path] = $branches;
22           }
23
24           // Since we've stripped whitespace, the result "* (detached from "
25 @@ -248,7 +254,7 @@ class Repository
26               $branches = array_slice($branches, 1);
27           }
28
29 -         return $branches;
30 +         return $cache[$this->path] = $branches;
```

```
31          }
32
33          /**
34  @@ -322,15 +328,21 @@ class Repository
35           */
36          public function getTags()
37          {
38  +           static $cache = array();
39  +
40  +           if (array_key_exists($this->path, $cache)) {
41  +               return $cache[$this->path];
42  +           }
43  +
44              $tags = $this->getClient()->run($this, "tag");
45              $tags = explode("\n", $tags);
46              array_pop($tags);
47
48              if (empty($tags[0])) {
49  -               return NULL;
50  +               return $cache[$this->path] = NULL;
51              }
52
53  -           return $tags;
54  +           return $cache[$this->path] = $tags;
55          }
56
57          /**
```

By now, you know the story by heart. Go to
https://fix2-ijtxpsladv67o.eu.platform.sh/Twig/, generate a profile with the
browser extension, and *compare it*[3] with the previous profile we made after the
first fix:

> *The profile is available at https://goo.gl/UOHQbo.*

 To find profiles on Blackfire's dashboard, look for the URL starting with
`fix1` and `fix2`. Blackfire also lets you **name your profiles** to find them
more easily. You can name a profile directly from the summary toolbar,
the dashboard, or the profile page.

And we did it again! 28% performance improvement on top of the 30%
improvement we had made before. We can confirm the overall speedup by
comparing the profile before any fixes with the latest one:

> *The profile is available at https://goo.gl/t9Qeyr.*

These two patches improve the performance of the GitList project page by *49%*
(from *118ms* to *60ms*).

---

3. `https://blackfire.io/profiles/compare/f3707234-afe3-4c35-aae0-a60f11f3add3/graph`

As *Gitter*[4], the project we optimized, is Open-Source, we've submitted a pull request with our findings and it has been merged.

Day-to-Day Profiling Methodology

To sum up, finding and fixing performance bottlenecks always uses the same profiling methodology:

- Profile key pages;
- Select the slowest ones;
- Compare and analyze profiles to spot differences and bottlenecks (on all dimensions);
- Find the biggest bottlenecks;
- Try to fix the issue or improve the overall performance;
- Check that tests are not broken;
- Generate a profile of the updated version of the code;
- Compare the new profile with the first one;
- Take a moment to celebrate your achievement;
- Rinse and repeat.

Conclusion

You might think that optimizing an application like we've just done is enough and that Blackfire is not needed anymore. And you would be wrong. This is just the beginning of our journey. Performance management is a day-to-day activity. Whenever you fix a bug or add a new feature in your application, you should check that you have not introduced a performance regression.

The next chapter will guide you through the installation of Blackfire on your environment to let you profile your very own projects.

---

4. https://github.com/klaussilveira/gitter

Chapter 6
Installation

Up until now, we have used the Blackfire browser extension to profile a project hosted on Blackfire servers. This was the easiest way to get us started, but now it's time for you to use Blackfire on your own projects.

Infrastructure

Blackfire is a SaaS product (an on Premise Edition is also available). The blackfire.io website allows you to manage your Blackfire project configurations, profiles, and builds. Still, you need to install some software:

- The **Blackfire PHP C extension**, the probe, instruments PHP code and gathers data about runtime behavior. The probe knows how and when to instrument the code, and how to extract data out of the PHP runtime.
- The **Blackfire agent** handles most of the intensive operations (like cleaning, anonymizing, and compressing the data) before sending each profile to Blackfire's servers. It uses a socket to communicate with the probe and HTTPS to send data to Blackfire.

When you are manually triggering Blackfire profiles, you will do so using one of the following tools:

- The **Blackfire companion** is a browser extension that makes it conveninent to generate profiles from the browser.
- The **Blackfire client**, which comes bundled with the agent, lets you generate profiles from the command line. It gives more flexibility and has more features than the companion and will be the covered in a future chapter.

Data Privacy

Blackfire servers store some data about your code execution. You can learn about data privacy in our FAQ and in this *blog post*[1].

Installation on your Local Computers

Blackfire is supported on many platforms. Install it by following the instructions for your operating system:

> The full instructions are available at *https://blackfire.io/docs/up-and-running/installation*.

Installation on Staging, Testing, and Production

When deploying code to testing, staging, or production environments, you can use the same installation procedure as in the previous section, or use Blackfire's integrations with Chef, Puppet, Ansible, or Docker.

Blackfire is also pre-installed on some platforms, such as Magento Commerce Cloud, *SymfonyCloud*[2] or Platform.sh. The configuration procedure might be a little different, please make sure to refer to those platform's documentation.

Next Steps

You are now ready to profile your very own projects!

First, validate your installation by generating a profile with the companion. If you have any problems, read our troubleshooting guide or contact our support.

Once you're able to generate a profile, use the profiling methodology we described in the previous chapters to run Blackfire on your applications. I'm very confident that for any non-trivial codebase, you will find some optimizations.

Found an optimization? Share it with us on Twitter and use the #blackfireio hashtag.

---

1. https://blog.blackfire.io/data-privacy-and-blackfire.html
2. https://symfony.com/cloud/

Chapter 7

Time Flavors

When talking about performance, time is probably the first dimension everyone thinks of. Time comes in several flavors, as you discovered when profiling your first requests. In that chapter we covered several types of time measurements (wall time, I/O time, and CPU time), but we did not discuss their differences or unpack why having multiple notions of time is important when analyzing a profile. The time has come!

Wall Clock Time

The **Wall Clock Time**, or **Wall Time**, for a function call is the measure of the *real time* it took for PHP to execute its code: the difference between the time at which PHP entered the function and the time at which PHP left the function.

The time it takes for PHP to execute some fragment of code depends on the resources it accesses: the number of instructions executed on the CPU, the amount of data read from memory, the time it took for network services to respond, the size of any files read from disk, etc. Each one of these activities incurs some overhead.

To keep things simple, wall time is usually split in two main parts: the **CPU Time** and the **I/O Time**.

CPU Time

The **CPU time** is the amount of time the CPU was used for **processing instructions**.

I/O Time

The **I/O time** is the time the **CPU waited for input/output** (I/O) operations.

We can divide I/O time into two parts: the **network** and the **disk**.

Network activity includes calls to databases like MySQL, PostreSQL, or MongoDB; HTTP calls to web services and APIs; calls to cache systems like Redis and Memcached; communications with services like queues, email daemons, remote filesystems; etc.

Disk activity occurs when a program reads files from the filesystem, including when PHP loads a script or class file.

 Keep in mind that the I/O time is almost never 0 as it includes some non-significant activities (like memory access).

CPU vs I/O

In summary:

Wall Time = CPU Time + I/O Time

I/O Time = Network Time + Disk Time

Why distinguish these types of times? Well, you've probably heard of a program being **I/O bound** or **CPU-bound**.

A **CPU-bound** program's speed depends mostly on the CPU. In other words, CPU utilization is high for long periods of time. The faster the CPU, the faster the code runs.

On the contrary, an **I/O bound** program's speed is determined by the time spent waiting for I/O. Faster disks or a faster network improve the overall performance of I/O bound code.

Being able to understand if a piece of code is CPU intensive or does a lot of I/O activity is a crucial part of finding the root cause of performance issues as it gives hints about what to look for.

Inclusive vs Exclusive Time

By now, you should you have a clear understanding of the different time flavors. But as reasoning on the global times is quite useless, Blackfire also attaches times to each function call. Allocating times is complex, so let's see how Blackfire does it with a simple example:

Listing 7-1
```
1   function foo()
2   {
3       $a = new Bar();
4       $count = $a->getCount();
```

```
5
6    $str = '';
7    for ($i = 0; $i < $count; $i++) {
8        $str .= str_repeat('foo', 10);
9    }
10
11   $str = $a->sanitizeString($str);
12
13   return $str;
14 }
15
16 echo foo();
```

When calling foo(), a node representing the consumed resources associated with this call is added in the call graph. The **inclusive time** of this function call is the time it took for PHP to execute all lines of code in the foo() method.

During the execution of foo(), two methods and one function are called: getCount(), sanitizeString(), and str_repeat(). Those three calls are represented as **child nodes** in the call graph under the foo() **parent node**. As discussed in a previous chapter, foo() has 3 **callees** and sanitizeString() has one **caller**. And getCount(), sanitizeString(), and str_repeat() also have their own **inclusive time**.

The foo() inclusive time includes the time it takes to execute the code within the function (like the for loop) but also the inclusive time for all its children. That's the reason why it's called the inclusive time.

 Blackfire makes no differences between PHP built-in method and function calls and userland calls; they are all represented as nodes. However, language constructs (like for, if, ...) are not represented as nodes.

The inclusive time allows you to find the critical path of an application. When you follow the functions with the highest inclusive time, you are going down the critical path. The critical path is where you need to look at when trying to assess an application performance.

What about the exclusive time then?

The **exclusive time** for a function call is the time spent in the function itself, **excluding time spent in child calls**. The exclusive time for the foo() function is highlighted in the code below:

Listing 7-2
```
1  function foo()
2  {
3      $a = new Bar();
4      $count =
5          $a->getCount();
6
7      $str = '';
8      for ($i = 0; $i < $count; $i++) {
9          $str .=
10             str_repeat('foo', 10);
11     }
```

```
12
13     $str =
14         $a->sanitizeString($str);
15
16     return $str;
17 }
```

The exclusive time allows finding the function calls to optimize first. It tells you which function calls consumed most of the resources by themselves.

Note that the exclusive/inclusive distinction can be made for all dimensions of a call graph: the time but also the memory, the network, ...

Conclusion

Time is a complex dimension, but hopefully you now have a better understanding of the different types of time you will see on a Blackfire call graph.

Chapter 8
Profiling all the Things

Ready to take it to the next level? Profiling HTTP GET requests is pretty cool, but you can use Blackfire to profile so much more: AJAX requests, form submissions, POST, PUT, and DELETE requests... you can even use Blackfire to profile CLI scripts.

Using the Blackfire Browser Extension

The browser extension's big red "Profile!" button is rather straight-forward to use.

Now click below it: "Profile all Requests". With a simple Start/Stop action, Blackfire will profile all the PHP requests which will be generated while you browse your website.

The icing on the cake: when we say "all requests", that means no matter what domain they are on! For instance, if an Ajax request in your application hits another domain where you installed Blackfire as well, that request will also be profiled!

Using the Blackfire CLI

Profiling complex requests or CLI scripts can also be done using the `blackfire` command line tool, which was installed along with the Blackfire agent in a previous chapter. Confirm that everything works fine by running the following command:

Listing 8-1

```
1   blackfire config --dump
```

You should see the current configuration with your `client-id` and `client-token` (if not, run `blackfire config` and use your personal client credentials).

Profiling HTTP Requests from the CLI

Let's profile the GitList homepage, but this time from the command line:

Listing 8-2

```
1  blackfire curl https://gitlist.demo.blackfire.io/
```

This command does the exact same thing as the browser extension, but from the command line: first you see a progress bar, followed by a profile summary and a link to the full profile:

Listing 8-3

```
1  Profiling: [####################################] 10/10
2  Blackfire cURL completed
3  Profile URL: https://blackfire.io/profiles/9ee9de4b-b086-4986-9d0b-53a9251001eb/
4  graph
5
6  Wall Time    14.7ms
7  CPU Time     10.6ms
8  I/O Time     4.06ms
9  Memory       1.66MB
   Network      n/a
```

 Under the hood, `blackfire curl` uses cURL to issue HTTP requests to your servers and therefore supports all cURL features, making it very powerful. You must have cURL installed in order for this to work.

You can also use **wget** or any other tools able to make HTTP requests, but the process is more manual as described later in this chapter.

Now, let's profile the GitList search engine, which is a POST request.

Go to `https://fix2-ijtxpsladv67o.eu.platform.sh/Twig/` in Google Chrome, open the "Network" tab of the Browser's Developer Tools (*View > Developer > Developer Tools*), and search for "loader" in the search box:

Look for the POST request sent by the browser by using the "Doc" filter (see the image above), right-click on the page name and select "Copy as cURL":

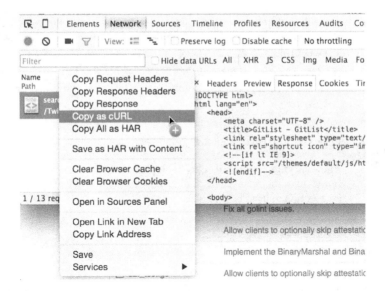

Using the browser to get the exact URL to profile is very convenient. Now, from your console, type "blackfire --samples=1" and paste the copied URL:

Listing 8-4

```
1  blackfire --samples=1 curl 'https://fix2-ijtxpsladv67o.eu.platform.sh/Twig/tree/
2  1.x/search' \
3      -H 'Origin: https://fix2-ijtxpsladv67o.eu.platform.sh' \
4      -H 'Accept-Encoding: gzip, deflate' \
5      -H 'Accept-Language: en-US,en;q=0.8,fr;q=0.6' \
6      -H 'Upgrade-Insecure-Requests: 1' \
7      -H 'User-Agent: Mozilla/5.0 (Macintosh; Intel Mac OS X 10_10_5) AppleWebKit/
8  537.36 (KHTML, like Gecko) Chrome/46.0.2490.86 Safari/537.36' \
9      -H 'Content-Type: application/x-www-form-urlencoded' \
10     -H 'Accept: text/html,application/xhtml+xml,application/xml;q=0.9,image/
    webp,*/*;q=0.8' \
       -H 'Cache-Control: max-age=0' -H 'Referer:
    https://fix2-ijtxpsladv67o.eu.platform.sh/Twig/' \
       -H 'Connection: keep-alive' -H 'DNT: 1' --data 'query=loader' --compressed
```

Note that using `--samples=1` is safer as it avoids running several iterations of a non-GET HTTP request that might have side effects.

The generated profile should look something like this:

The profile is available at https://goo.gl/AFzb7h.

The **Process** runs take most of the time but the `Twig_Template::getAttribute()` method is called 2500+ times for 13% of the total time. `Twig_Template::getAttribute()` being the bottleneck is typical of a Twig application. Could the *Twig C extension*[1] improve the performance? It depends... who knows? Probably? We are using Blackfire now, so we know. **Stop guessing and measure**. Make an informed decision.

---

1. https://twig.symfony.com/doc/1.x/installation.html#installing-the-c-extension

That's the typical workflow for non-GET HTTP requests like POST requests or Ajax requests. As an exercise, generate a profile for the Ajax requests sent when going to the Twig project "Network" page.

Profiling HTTP APIs is no different from profiling regular HTTP web requests, but a tool like *httpie* might simplify commands a lot. Read how you can use httpie with Blackfire.

Generate JSON representation of Profiles and Comparisons

The Blackfire command line tool `--json` option outputs a JSON representation of profiles and comparisons. It allows for simple automation tools to be developed on top of Blackfire.

Profiling CLI Commands

The Blackfire command line tool can be used to profile PHP CLI scripts via the `run` command:

Listing 8-5

```
1  blackfire run php -r 'echo "Hello World!";'
```

The output looks like before:

Listing 8-6

```
1   Hello World!
2
3   Blackfire Run completed
4   Profile URL: https://blackfire.io/profiles/01e44337-ae51-465b-95ce-fb5fff3f73b7/
5   graph
6
7   Wall Time     399µs
8   CPU Time      395µs
9   I/O Time       4µs
10  Memory        66.9KB
    Network        n/a
```

The call graph for this profile is not that interesting but notice that "Hello World!" is displayed only once. By default, Blackfire only runs the code once for command line scripts. You can change this behavior using the `--samples` option:

Listing 8-7

```
1  blackfire --samples=5 run php -r 'echo "Hello World!";'
```

To make profiling from the command line more exciting, let's run PHP Mess detector on Twig. PHP Mess Detector is a nice static analysis tool that tries to find potential problems in your code by using the raw metrics measured by PHP Depend.

Download phpmd version 2.2.1[2] as a phar, and execute it on the Twig source code like this:

---

2. https://static.phpmd.org/php/2.2.1/phpmd.phar

Listing 8-8

```
1   blackfire run php phpmd.phar /path/to/Twig/lib/ text cleancode
2
3   Blackfire Run completed
4   Profile URL: https://blackfire.io/profiles/452155e7-435b-438d-a84e-3249ee1cfafa/
5   graph
6
7   Wall Time      18.1s
8   CPU Time       17.7s
9   I/O Time       441ms
10  Memory         42MB
    Network        n/a
```

> **blackfire run** supports any methods of running PHP scripts, from the standard **php script.php**, to using phars and executable scripts via a shebang (i.e. **#!/usr/bin/env php**).

If you run the command again, the code is going to run a lot faster, around 9 seconds, as phpmd uses a cache by default, stored under **~/.pdepend**. This second run is our baseline.

Can we do better than 9 seconds? You've probably already spotted three potential issues: the **unserialize()** function is called 4,500+ times, and these calls account for more than two-thirds of the inclusive time. As **unserialize()** is a built-in PHP function, its exclusive time cannot be optimized. What about its children? The **ASTNode::__wakeup()** method is called 825,000+ times and the special "Garbage Collection" node takes 20% of the total time.

> Blackfire is the only PHP profiler that gives detailed information about PHP garbage collector behavior.

As we cannot modify the **.phar** file easily, clone the phpmd repository and run Composer to install its dependencies:

Listing 8-9

```
1   git clone https://github.com/phpmd/phpmd.git
2   cd phpmd
3   git checkout -b 2.2.1 2.2.1
4   composer install
```

By default, the **src/bin/phpmd** script uses an in-memory cache, so switch to the file cache strategy used by the phar file by editing the **pdepend.xml.dist** configuration file:

Listing 8-10

```
1   diff --git a/pdepend.xml.dist b/pdepend.xml.dist
2   index 5d02cd2..384e827 100644
3   --- a/pdepend.xml.dist
4   +++ b/pdepend.xml.dist
5   @@ -5,7 +5,7 @@
6       xsi:schemaLocation="http://symfony.com/schema/dic/services http://symfony.com/
7   schema/dic/services/services-1.0.xsd">
8       <config>
9           <cache>
```

```
10    -             <driver>memory</driver>
11    +             <driver>file</driver>
12              </cache>
          </config>
```

Time to create a profile, after having primed the cache:

Listing 8-11
```
1    # prime the cache
2    php src/bin/phpmd /path/to/Twig/lib/ text cleancode
3
4    # create a profile
5    blackfire run php src/bin/phpmd /path/to/Twig/lib/ text cleancode
6
7    Blackfire Run completed
8    Profile URL: https://blackfire.io/profiles/f2ac6fc7-5c81-415d-97a6-49249a88abe6/
9    graph
10
11   Wall Time      9.27s
12   CPU Time       8.86s
13   I/O Time       412ms
14   Memory         40MB
     Network        n/a
```

Adding a cache to `FileCacheDriver::restoreFile()`, the `unserialize()` parent, avoids the unserialization of the same content over and over again:

Listing 8-12
```
1    index dedde40..3ae43d9 100644
2    --- a/src/main/php/PDepend/Util/Cache/Driver/FileCacheDriver.php
3    +++ b/src/main/php/PDepend/Util/Cache/Driver/FileCacheDriver.php
4    @@ -180,11 +180,17 @@ class FileCacheDriver implements CacheDriver
5        */
6        public function restore($key, $hash = null)
7        {
8    +       static $cache = array();
9    +
10   +       if (array_key_exists($key.'__'.$hash, $cache)) {
11   +           return $cache[$key.'__'.$hash];
12   +       }
13   +
14          $file = $this->getCacheFile($key);
15          if (file_exists($file)) {
16   -           return $this->restoreFile($file, $hash);
17   +           return $cache[$key.'__'.$hash] = $this->restoreFile($file, $hash);
18          }
19   -       return null;
20   +       return $cache[$key.'__'.$hash] = null;
21       }
22
23       /**
```

After applying the patch, generate a new profile:

Listing 8-13
```
1    blackfire run php src/bin/phpmd /path/to/Twig/lib/ text cleancode
2
3    Blackfire Run completed
4    Profile URL: https://blackfire.io/profiles/a41fd400-a3b6-492f-996f-38e2638f5327/
5    graph
6
7    Wall Time      3.8s
```

```
 8   CPU  Time    3.42s
 9   I/O  Time    383ms
10   Memory        68MB
     Network        n/a
```

Go to your Blackfire dashboard and compare the two profiles. You can see that **the trade-off for having a faster code is a significant memory consumption increase**. On the call graph, check that the main source of performance gains indeed comes from the drastic reduction of the number of `unseralize()` calls.

The other possible optimization comes from the special "Garbage Collection" node, which aggregates the resources consumed by PHP garbage collector. The garbage collection runs were not able to free up any memory (memory is 0 in the node details), so disabling it (via **-d zend.enable_gc=0** on the CLI or **gc_disable()** in the PHP code) should be safe and should make our code even faster:

Listing 8-14

```
 1   blackfire run php -d zend.enable_gc=0 src/bin/phpmd /path/to/Twig/lib/ text
 2   cleancode
 3
 4   Blackfire Run completed
 5   Profile URL: https://blackfire.io/profiles/342ef846-1de2-465c-bdf6-ef71bfb494c3/
 6   graph
 7
 8   Wall Time    2.54s
 9   CPU  Time    2.19s
10   I/O  Time    346ms
     Memory       68.1MB
     Network       n/a
```

Indeed, this makes our code much faster without any memory consumption increase:

The profile is available at https://goo.gl/KhofcH.

If you want to learn more about how garbage collecting works in PHP, please read *Anthony Ferrara's very detailed blog post*[3].

You might be thinking that adding some cache is the only fix that can optimize an application, but that's just because we have chosen our examples for their simplicity and the small code changes needed to make them faster.

In modern web applications, the common fixes are the reduction of the number of SQL queries and the number of external HTTP requests (API calls). Avoiding running the same code more than once is always a good idea anyway, and Blackfire lets you spot those occurrences. The inclusion of SQL queries and HTTP requests in your profiles is part of Blackfire's premium and enterprise offerings and will be discussed in a coming chapter.

---

3. https://blog.ircmaxell.com/2014/12/what-about-garbage.html

Profiling consumers and daemons

Profiling consumers and daemons is a totally different story as they run for a very long period of time. Auto-instrumentation, as done by Blackfire by default, cannot work in these cases. This is a topic for a future chapter, as we first need to learn about manually instrumenting your code.

How does Blackfire work?

Nobody likes using "magic" tools, at least not developers. At first, you probably thought Blackfire was magic because of some unasked and unanswered questions. How does Blackfire know when to instrument your code?

Would you like to understand how Blackfire works behind the scene? Read on. If you don't like seeing magicians reveal their tricks, you can safely jump to the next section.

The main task of the browser extension and the blackfire command line tool is to trigger a profile by modifying the HTTP request or the CLI command, which in turns enables code instrumentation.

For HTTP requests, Blackfire adds a header, **X-Blackfire-Query**. The header value contains the profile configuration (like the number of samples, ...) and a signature that identifies the user triggering the profile.

For CLI scripts, Blackfire defines an environment variable, **BLACKFIRE_QUERY**, and its value is the same as for HTTP requests.

When populating this HTTP header or environment variable, Blackfire appends a signature generated by Blackfire's servers. When a request is received by your servers (or a command line script is run), the very first job of Blackfire's PHP extension is to check this signature. If the signature is invalid or the user is not authorized to run a profile (or if the value is missing altogether), instrumentation is disabled. To avoid leaking the fact that Blackfire is installed, the PHP request is handled as if nothing happened.

In a nutshell, **Blackfire overhead is negligible except when a profile is requested** with an authorized signature in which case instrumentation is activated.

Using **wget** or any other HTTP tool instead of **curl** is no different. As **blackfire run** defines the **BLACKFIRE_QUERY** environment variable, use it to populate the **X-Blackfire-Query** header:

```
1  # replace blackfire curl
2  blackfire run sh -c 'curl -H "X-Blackfire-Query: $BLACKFIRE_QUERY"
3  http://example.com/ > /dev/null'
4
5  # use wget instead of cURL
   blackfire run sh -c 'wget --header="X-Blackfire-Query: $BLACKFIRE_QUERY"
   http://example.com/ > /dev/null'
```

Listing 8.15

For HTTP APIs, try *httpie* as a great alternative to cURL:

```
1   blackfire run sh -c 'http --json PUT example.org name=Fabien
    "X-Blackfire-Query:$BLACKFIRE_QUERY" > /dev/null'
```

A Word about Security

Blackfire signatures use a public/private key cryptographic system; the signatures use *Ed25519 cryptography*[4]. Ed25519 generates short signatures that are embedded in HTTP headers while ensuring state-of-the-art security and performance (more about security in our *Blackfire Security Model*[5] blog post).

Auto Instrumentation

No code change is needed to enable Blackfire. Everything happens from the outside as explained in the previous section.

Auto-instrumentation is very convenient, but it also allows Blackfire to profile way more than any other profiler as it can hook into the PHP engine very early on and stop the instrumentation very late; just a few examples of what Blackfire can profile thanks to auto-instrumentation: destructors, the PHP garbage collector, sessions, PHP file compilations, OPcache, and more.

Conclusion

The Blackfire command line tool is the best way to profile any PHP code and do some basic automation. The Profiling CLI Commands and Profiling HTTP Requests cookbooks are a good reference for all supported options.

Time again to profile your own applications and see if you can find some more bottlenecks. If you get stuck making sense of the call graph, that's the topic of the next chapter.

---

4. https://ed25519.cr.yp.to/
5. https://blog.blackfire.io/credentials.html

Chapter 9
Call Graphs Galore

In the previous chapters, we analyzed some call graphs, but we never fully explained what they represent and how to read them efficiently. Let's dive into the wonderful world of call graphs.

Call Graphs

Blackfire **records the functions called during the execution of a program and their relationships** as a call graph. A call graph knows nothing about when a function was called, but it reports the sequence of calls between functions.

In a call graph, **nodes represent functions and edges the calls between them**:

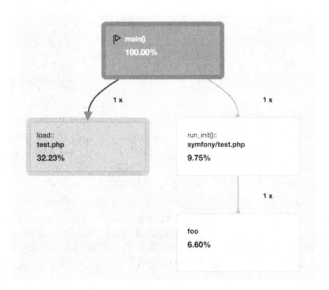

A node that has one or more children is called a **caller** for these child nodes; a node that has a parent is called a **callee** of this parent node.

 When we refer to a "function call" in this chapter, it can be a call to a PHP function (foo()), a method call on an object ($foo->bar()), or a static method call on a class (Foo::bar()).

To keep data small, Blackfire **does not keep the full-context** of calls (i.e. the arguments). Therefore, a node aggregates all calls to a function, regardless of the argument values. This is why each node has a count (the number of times the function was called) and why nodes can have more than one parent.

For some specific functions, Blackfire does **keep one argument at most** to gather useful generic information like SQL queries, HTTP requests, or specific information like the event name for the Symfony event dispatcher. In that case, specific nodes are created for each unique argument.

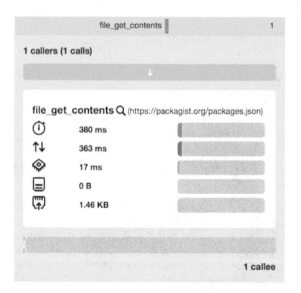

 Having only one node for each function call greatly simplifies the interpretation. But keep in mind that functions for which we gather an argument consist of several nodes (using the search engine helps figure that out), like for the file_get_contents() example above.

When generating a call graph, Blackfire does not cycle through the same node multiple times for recursive calls. Instead, it creates additional nodes for each recursive call and suffixes those nodes with @n. This type of graph, called an **acyclic graph**, is much easier to read and makes calculating exclusive costs much simpler.

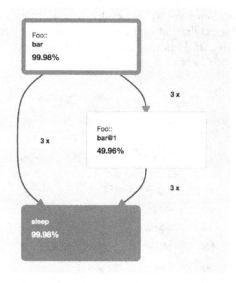

A Blackfire call graph is selective in what it displays. When you profile an application with many, many function calls, you will not see so many nodes on the graph. This is because Blackfire **cleans up the data**. Small nodes (function calls that consume negligible resources) are hidden by default. However, you will see these minor nodes when you focus the graph on a caller or a callee, as all parents and children of the focused node are always displayed.

Blackfire also removes nodes that are too small to be optimized. They are represented in the functions table as a grey bar:

Blackfire also **adds some special nodes** that are not function calls per se like the main node, garbage collection, and session serialization. These nodes augment the call graph with useful information that helps us understand PHP's behavior while executing your code:

Data Anonymization

The call graph data sent to Blackfire's server is thoroughly sanitized and never contains sensitive data. Function names do not convey any meaningfulness without their associated code, and arguments are anonymized by the agent before they are sent to our servers (SQL arguments are removed; usernames, passwords, and query arguments are removed from HTTP requests, etc).

If you want to inspect the traffic between your profiled server and Blackfire's servers, you can check the transmitted data by using our free and transparent proxy. Please read the instructions in the script itself.

Extra Features

Blackfire's user interface has many additional features that make navigating your call graph a breeze:

- The **SQL queries** and **HTTP requests** are available in the main toolbar:

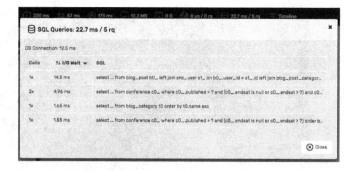

- The **search engine** allows you to search for specific function names. It can also be used to display all calls coming from a specific class or namespace:

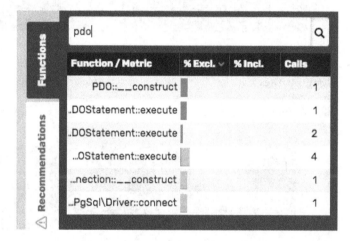

- In the top left of the call graph, hover on the profile title to reveal all its **metadata** (the URL or the command that was profiled but also alerts like when was experiencing high load during the profiling session), and additional cache usage information:

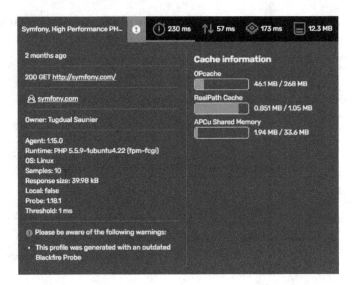

- In the top right corner of the call graph, the sharing icon allows you to **share profiles** with anybody (be warned that shared profiles are public and anyone can access them; note that for sensitive call graphs, you can also collaborate on profiles privately by using Blackfire's environments):

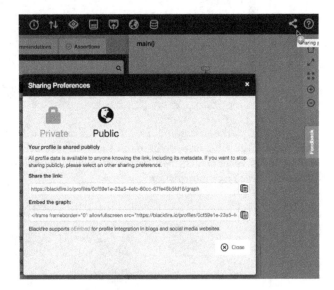

Call Graph Analyzing Methodology

Looking at a call graph can be overwhelming. Where do you start? What are you looking for first? When do you stop?

The goal of any profiling session is to find the function calls or the group of function calls that **consume the most resources** and then be able to analyze their implementation and find ways to optimize them.

Don't forget one of Blackfire's core tenets:

Knowing when to stop optimizing is as important as knowing where to start.

The goal when profiling an application is never to optimize everything. Instead, Blackfire helps you find areas of your application to optimize that will give you the best improvements. That's exactly what we have done in the previous chapters. We were able to significantly optimize two Open-Source projects by applying some changes that were easy to apply once we knew where to look.

Focusing the Call Graph

All these methodologies help you find the function calls you need to optimize first. Whatever the methodology, when you find such a call, always focus on the corresponding node in the Blackfire interface so that you can see more context in the call graph. You can focus on a node from the call graph or from the function list by clicking on the magnifying glass:

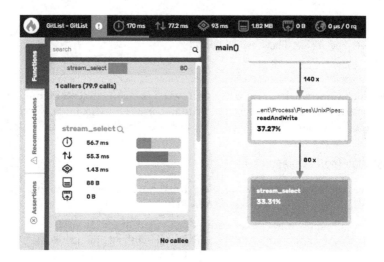

The call graph is then centered around the selected function call and all callers and callees are displayed, even the smaller ones. This view gives you more context to understand the real behavior of the code.

There are two main approaches to analyzing a call graph: the **function calls first approach**, and the **call graph top/down approach**. Both methods are complementary.

Remember that all methodologies apply to any dimension: call time, I/O time, CPU time, memory, and network.

Function Calls First Approach

This method involves looking first at the function table on the left side of the Blackfire interface.

First, **sort the table by exclusive time** (default sort), and focus on functions **in the top 25 only**, in this order of importance:

- calls coming from your code;
- calls coming from third-party PHP libraries (you might submit a patch upstream quite as we've done in previous chapters).

Then, **sort the table by number of calls** and look for the same functions as above adding one more type:

- calls coming from PHP built-in functions or C extensions (the number of calls is probably the only way to improve their performance).

 Never try to optimize a function with a high call count if its overall cost is negligible. This is never worth it.

This technique works great when there are a few calls that stand out; These cases are usually caused by developer mistakes (n + 1 queries, intensive function calls that could have been cached, large number of calls of a single function, ...).

Call Graph Top/Down Approach

This method involves **following the critical path** on the call graph to better understand how the code is executed by PHP.

On the call graph, the critical path is composed of all the nodes with a red border. Start at the `main` node, then follow its children by navigating the call graph with the mouse.

Whenever you encounter several branches, choose the branch that mostly involves function calls coming from your codebase.

Then, stop when a node looks like it could be optimized (i.e. if you see a significant drop in exclusive time).

This technique works well when it is not immediately obvious where to focus first. Also, once you find a node to look at more closely, you already have a better understanding of the context and what happened before.

Instead of following the call graph, you can perform the same technique directly from the function calls table by sorting it by **inclusive time**.

Checking the Cache Configuration

Correctly configuring PHP caches is critical for optimal performance: you should not get to a full cache. Anytime you profile your code, when viewing the profile data, hover on the profile name to view the cache information.

RealPath Cache

The `realpath()` function returns the absolute path for any given relative file path. This conversion takes a non-negligible time because it performs some filesystem calls. That's why PHP caches the results of `realpath()` calls and their associated `stat()` calls. The `realpath_cache_size` ini setting defines the size of this cache.

The realpath cache is only used for file paths that exist and is used for most of PHP filesystem calls. Complex applications involve a lot of file operations, so this cache size must be increased accordingly.

Interned Strings

Interned strings are a nice memory optimization that was added in PHP 5.4.

PHP stores immutable strings (a `char *`) into a special buffer to be able to reuse its pointer for all occurrences of the same string. This `setting` can be adjusted using the `opcache.interned_strings_buffer`.

Conclusion

One last bit of advice. Optimization is often a trade-off of **time versus memory** and **performance versus code complexity**. Sometimes, it is better to keep a slower implementation to preserve a simpler and more readable codebase. Blackfire is just a tool, don't apply a methodology blindly.

Blackfire provides a rich user interface that lets developers navigate through function calls to efficiently find performance issues.

Profiling should not always be a lonely activity. Teamwork often helps makes finding problems and writing fixes go more quickly. Blackfire helps achieve better collaboration through environments, which is the topic for the next chapter.

Chapter 10
Collaborating via Environments

When you got started with Blackfire, you used your Blackfire personal client and server credentials to profile local projects. It was the best way to configure Blackfire on your personal computer.

But what about enabling a team of developers to diagnose problems on production servers? Or configuring Blackfire on a Continuous Integration server? Blackfire is not just useful on a development server, but also on testing, staging, and production servers.

If you were to use your personal server credentials on a shared server, you would be the only one able to profile projects hosted on it. Another developer in your team trying to generate a profile would be rejected as their client credentials would generate a signature that would not match the server credentials. This is the Blackfire security mechanism that protects your servers from unauthorized activities.

Fortunately, Blackfire supports another way to configure shared servers. **Environments** let teams of developers manage the performance of various servers via common server credentials. **An environment is a workspace** where generated profiles are only accessible to team members.

 Environments are more than just a set of credentials. This feature also allows a team to configure workflows and business logic depending on the server and app on which you collaborate. You can configure specific assertions, test scenarios, scenario triggers, and notifications. Environments give you access to SQL queries and outgoing HTTP request details, as well as longer data retention. Environments also gives you access to quality and security recommendations. These topics will be discussed in a later chapter.

Environments are part of our Premium and Enterprise offerings. If you haven't yet, consider starting a *free Premium trial*[1] so you can follow along with this chapter and the next ones (no credit card required).

---

1. https://blackfire.io/try/premium

If your Premium trial is already finished, the team will be happy to consider resetting it for you. Reach out to the *support*[2].

Why use Environments?

A single environment can be used on an unlimited number of servers, projects, and domain names. What's more, it is possible to use more than one set of credentials on a single server. So why would anyone ever create more than one environment?

The main usages for environments are the following:

- **Access control**: Authorize specific groups of users to profile specific servers.
- **Profile management**: Isolate profiles under one workspace. Comparing profiles coming from development machines (logging and debugging are enabled and caching is disabled) and profiles from production servers can lead to confusing comparisons and misguided conclusions.
- **Configuration**: Optimize configuration depending on the server usage. In production you will want to receive an urgent notification if a performance issue is detected, whereas a simple email may be sufficient if the same issue is detected in your continuous integration environment. The way you trigger performance tests can also be different: for every pull requests for testing or on a scheduled basis for production.

One best practice is to **create several environments per project**: one for testing, one for staging, and one for production. At the end of the day, it is up to you to decide how to organize your environments depending on your infrastructure and the way you work.

For development computers, you should use personal server credentials as they have an exclusive feature: they allow you to profile all environments you have access to without switching credentials. However, you may want to create a specific environment for development as well if you are using a project-specific Vagrant box or Docker images shared by all developers.

Creating Environments

Create an environment by clicking on "Create Environment" from the My Environments tab. Give your new environment a name, a description (describe what it gives access to for instance), and optionally a canonical URL.

---

2. https://support.blackfire.io/

On the environment page, give access to some developers by inviting them via the "Settings" tab:

Lastly, configure your server with the server credentials from the "Settings" tab (more on that in the next section):

Configuring Environments

The easiest way to set up credentials on your server is to paste them into the Blackfire agent's configuration file, which is probably what you have done on your personal computer. It works great for standard setups where a server hosts only one project and the agent is configured locally.

Server credentials can also be configured in various other ways, depending on your hosting strategy: you can use them to secure **multiple projects on one server** or **one project on a farm of servers**. Blackfire supports these use cases and more, thanks to the following abilities:

- An agent does not have to be installed on the same server as the PHP stack. The PHP C extension can communicate with the agent via either a file **or** TCP socket. You can install one agent on a dedicated server and connect it to all of your web servers;
- Server credentials can also be configured via environment variables. Define these environment variables in your web server configuration (i.e. per virtual host) or define environment variables in your console when using the Blackfire command-line tool;
- Server credentials can be configured in the PHP configuration file (`php.ini`), allowing you to set up different credential per PHP-FPM pool.

The Configuration chapter in the reference guide describes how this works in practice.

Conclusion

Blackfire environments are a great way to collaborate on profiling activities. They give you a lot of flexibility in terms of configuration and access management.

We have mentioned assertions and scenarios in this chapter. Now that you have access to these features via the Premium trial, it is time to go beyond profiling. **Blackfire is much more than a profiler**, and the next chapter will continue our journey with Blackfire assertions.

Chapter 11

Writing Assertions

This series started by making the case that performance should be considered a feature of your application. Like any feature, performance should be well-tested, but how can you write tests on a profile call graph? This is yet another unique Blackfire feature.

Testing Profiles Main Costs

Remember the first GitList profiles you generated with Blackfire? We discovered that a project page is much slower than the homepage (around 100ms versus 20ms). Checking that PHP never takes more than 50ms to render a GitList web page can be expressed with the following **Blackfire assertion**:

Listing 11-1

```
1    main.wall_time < 50ms
```

What about making sure memory usage never grows beyond 2Mb? Here you go:

Listing 11-2

```
1    main.memory < 2Mb
```

Like xUnit test frameworks, Blackfire groups related assertions in **tests**. Tests are written in the YAML format and stored in a `.blackfire.yml` file in your project's root directory or one of its parent:

Listing 11-3

```
1    # .blackfire.yml
2    tests:
3        "All pages are fast":
4            path: "/.*"
5            assertions:
6                - main.wall_time < 50ms
7                - main.memory < 2Mb
```

You can create a new test by adding an entry in the **tests** block. Give it a name ("All pages are fast") and configure it with a **path**, the HTTP path info that must match for the **assertions** to be evaluated.

The .blackfire.yml file must be stored in your project alongside the project code for the same reasons your unit and functional tests are stored with the code: Tests must evolve at the same time as the code. When adding a new feature or changing existing code, you should also add new Blackfire tests or update existing ones. Keeping everything together makes incorporating Blackfire into your development workflow much easier.

After creating the .blackfire.yml file, generate a new profile for the *GitList homepage*[1] and notice the new green tick in the browser profile summary:

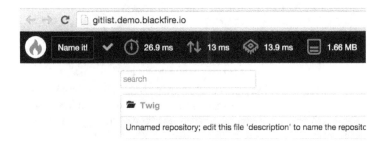

Do the same with the *Twig project homepage*[2] and you should see a red cross. When viewing the associated profile, select the "Assertions" tab to better understand which assertions failed and why:

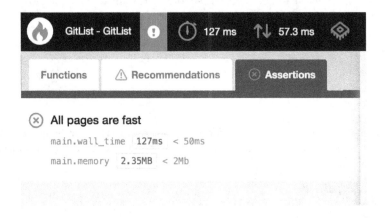

Evaluated assertions contain the actual values of all metrics and variables so that you can know how far away your code is from the expected value. For the profile above, the expected wall time was 50ms, while the actual wall time was 127ms.

---

1. https://gitlist.demo.blackfire.io/
2. https://gitlist.demo.blackfire.io/Twig/

Whenever a profile is generated for a new page or for a page where a bug was fixed or a new feature added, Blackfire will run all appropriate tests. The red cross or green tick will immediately tell you if any assertions failed.

To writing assertions on the main profile costs, add a valid dimension name to the `main.` prefix:

> The full list of available dimensions are available at *https://blackfire.io/docs/reference-guide/metrics#built-in-metrics*.

Testing Nodes

Testing the main profile dimensions is a good place to start, but Blackfire gathers much more data, including function calls and their associated costs. You can write tests against these statistics as well.

Assertions cannot be written on nodes directly, but via associated metrics. A **metric** is a name put on a node or a set of nodes that represents their costs. In assertions, **the value of a metric for a given dimension** can be used to define the performance expectations of a project.

Blackfire defines metrics for many built-in PHP features, popular PHP libraries, and the main PHP C extensions. Add the following Twig and Symfony related tests to your GitList `.blackfire.yml` file:

```yaml
1   tests:
2       "All pages are fast":
3           path: "/.*"
4           assertions:
5               - main.wall_time < 50ms
6               - main.memory < 2Mb
7
8       "Twig displays and renders":
9           path: "/.*"
10          assertions:
11              - metrics.twig.display.count + metrics.twig.render.count < 5
12
13      "Symfony events dispatched":
14          path: "/.*"
15          assertions:
16              - metrics.symfony.events.count < 10
```

Listing 11-4

Generating a profile on the Twig project homepage leads to the following results:

⊗ All pages are fast

main.wall_time `151ms` < 50ms

main.memory `2.36MB` < 2Mb

⊘ Twig displays

metrics.twig.display.count `0` +

metrics.twig.render.count `1` < 5

⊘ Symfony events dispatched

metrics.symfony.events.count `6` < 10

Metrics can have a direct relationship with a specific node like the number of Symfony event dispatched: the `metrics.symfony.events` metric contains the costs of the calls on the `Symfony\Component\EventDispatcher\EventDispatcher::dispatch()` method. But sometimes, like for the number of Twig template displays, it can be an aggregation of nodes:

Listing 11-5

```
 1  twig.display:
 2    label: "Number of Twig templates displayed"
 3    layer: ~
 4    matching_calls:
 5      php:
 6        - callee: "=twig_include"
 7          contrib: "count-only"
 8        - caller: "=Twig_Template::display"
 9          callee: "^Twig_Template__"
10          contrib: "count-only"
11        - caller: "=Twig_Template::display"
12          callee: "^block_"
13          contrib: "count-only"
```

 The format of metric definitions is defined in the metrics documentation.

Testing Comparisons

Blackfire tests are a great way to make sure that your application satisfies predefined performance constraints. You can also **check the evolution of the performance** by writing assertions for profile comparisons.

Assertions on comparisons ensure that an application's performance does not degrade from one version to the next. And then, when it crosses the threshold defined in your tests, fixing the problems will be more difficult and time-consuming.

For instance, you can limit the increase of memory from one version to the next with the following assertions:

Listing 11-6

```
1  # new version should not consume more than 10% more memory
2  percent(main.memory) < 10%
3
4  # new version should not consume more than 300kb of memory
5  diff(main.memory) < 300kb
```

Our final .blackfire.yml looks like this:

Listing 11-7

```
1  tests:
2      "All pages are fast":
3          path: "/.*"
4          assertions:
5              - main.wall_time < 50ms
6              - main.memory < 2Mb
7
8      "Twig displays":
9          path: "/.*"
10         assertions:
11             - metrics.twig.display.count + metrics.twig.render.count < 5
12
13     "Symfony events dispatched":
14         path: "/.*"
15         assertions:
16             - metrics.symfony.events.count < 10
17
18     "Memory evolution":
19         path: "/.*"
20         assertions:
21             - percent(main.memory) < 10%
22             - diff(main.memory) < 300kb
```

Comparing the GitList homepage with the Twig project homepage gives the following results:

⊗ All pages are fast

```
main.wall_time   366ms   < 50ms
main.memory   2.36MB   < 2Mb
```

⊘ Twig displays

```
metrics.twig.display.count   0   +
metrics.twig.render.count   1   < 5
```

⊘ Symfony events dispatched

```
metrics.symfony.events.count   6   < 10
```

⊗ Memory evolution

```
percent(main.memory   1.71MB ~> 2.36MB )  < 10%
diff(main.memory   1.71MB ~> 2.36MB )  < 300kb
```

Testing with Custom Metrics

Blackfire comes with many built-in metrics, but you can also create your own.

GitList makes extensive use of sub-processes to run Git commands. The main performance optimization we did was to reduce the number of executed Git commands. One possible test could be to check the number of sub-processes executed for any GitList page. As Blackfire does not come with a built-in metric for that, let's create one:

```
1  metrics:
2      process:
3          label: Process Calls
4          matching_calls:
5              php:
6                  - callee: '=Symfony\Component\Process\Process::start'
7
8  tests:
9      "Process calls":
10         path: "/.*"
11         assertions:
12             - metrics.process.count < 10
13             - metrics.process.wall_time < 30ms
```

Listing 11-8

Custom metrics are configured and used in the exact same way as built-in ones. The **process** metric aggregates the costs of all **Symfony\Component\Process\ Process::start()** method calls. The new test asserts that there are no more than 10 calls and that they do not take more than 30ms to execute:

⊗ Process calls

```
metrics.process.count    20  < 10

metrics.process.wall_time   28.1ms  < 30ms
```

⊗ All pages are fast

```
main.wall_time   168ms  < 50ms

main.memory   2.37MB  < 2Mb
```

⊘ Twig displays

```
metrics.twig.display.count   0  +
metrics.twig.render.count   1  < 5
```

⊘ Symfony events dispatched

```
metrics.symfony.events.count   6  < 10
```

The SQL queries and fetched URLs included in a Blackfire profile come from the graph as well. These values are arguments to specific function calls. Custom metrics can also get one argument per function call. For processes, it could be interesting to group calls by the command that was executed. The start() method does not take the command line as an argument, but the Process constructor does. Create a new metric whose only goal is to capture the first argument of the Process constructor:

Listing 11-9

```
1  metrics:
2    process_args:
3      label: Process Call Arguments
4      matching_calls:
5        php:
6          - callee:
7              selector: '=Symfony\Component\Process\Process::__construct'
8              argument: { 1: "^" }
```

If you generate a new profile, the command executed by the process is now part of the graph.

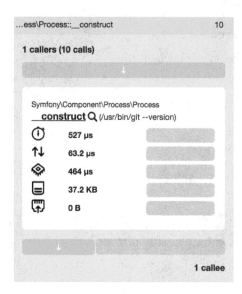

With this new metric in place we can see that running `git --version` 10 times is a waste of resources.

 When you configure Blackfire to gather an argument, the related nodes are always displayed, even if their consumed resources are insignificant as in the above example.

And we have just scratched the surface of what's possible with custom Blackfire metrics!

 The format of metric definitions is defined in the metrics documentation.

Testing CLI Commands

Testing CLI commands can be done in the `.blackfire.yml` file as well by replacing `path` with `command` in the test definition.

To optimize phpmd a few chapters ago, we made sure that `restoreFile()` was only called twice for each parsed file: once to retrieve the cache for the class itself and once to retrieve the cache for all its methods. The performance issue came from the fact that the cache for methods was retrieved the same number of times as the number of methods in the class instead of just once.

Let's write a test to check that the number of calls to `restoreFile()` to retrieve the cache for methods is exactly the same as the number of classes in the project phpmd is working on:

Listing 11-10

```
 1   metrics:
 2       parses:
 3           label: PHParser parses
 4           matching_calls:
 5               php:
 6                   - callee: '=PDepend\Source\Language\PHP\AbstractPHPParser::parse'
 7
 8       cache_driver:
 9           label: Restore files
10           matching_calls:
11               php:
12                   - callee:
13                       selector: '=PDepend\Util\Cache\Driver\
14   FileCacheDriver::restoreFile'
15                       argument: { 1: /methods/ }
16
17   tests:
18       "Cache works":
19           command: ".*"
20           assertions:
21               - metrics.parses.count == metrics.cache_driver.count
```

The first custom metric (**parses**) stores the number of classes to parse and the second one (**cache_driver**) stores the number of calls to **restoreFile()**, but only when the argument contains **methods** (methods are cached to files with names that include the string **methods**). The assertion is then a matter of checking that the two numbers are equal:

✓ Cache works

$$\text{metrics.parses.count} \quad \boxed{185} \quad ==$$
$$\text{metrics.cache\_driver.count} \quad \boxed{185}$$

You probably won't write this sort of test very often, but it demonstrates the simplicity and the expressiveness of Blackfire tests.

Conclusion

Blackfire tests use a rich expression language that allows developers to express any kind of assertion. Tests can be used for:

- defining a project performance reference;
- testing code's behavior;
- ensuring that there are no performance regressions.

Finding the right assertions for a project can be tough at first. In the next chapter we will discuss some best practices that will help you get started on the right foot.

Chapter 12

Forget about Time in your Tests

Writing good assertions is a difficult task. The easiest test you can think of probably involves the wall time or the memory, but assertions on these dimensions are actually very weak. **Time is not a stable metric**. External factors such as machine load can have significant impacts on wall time between two profiles of identical code. Volatile tests must be avoided at all costs as they make your test suite less reliable and degrade the trust your team has in any failures.

Forget about Time

Avoid writing assertions that depend on time. When running a piece of code, **time is just a consequence** of what happened in the code. Look deeper. Understanding which functions were called at runtime is exactly what a profiler is good at.

Use time to identify the slow parts in your code and then write assertions on the root cause.

A typical example is a microservice architecture where the number of HTTP requests on external web services is likely to be the main performance issue. The more HTTP requests you have in the code, the slower the code is going to be. The number of external requests is a stable value and it should not change between two profiles generated from the same codebase. Thus, limiting the number of HTTP requests allowed for a project is a great way to ensure good code performance:

Listing 12.1
```
1  # fragile, might break from time to time
2  - main.wall_time < 50ms
3
4  # robust, the real root cause for slowness
5  - metrics.http.requests.count < 5
```

Tests Best Practices

We already used such an approach when we wrote assertions for GitList and phpmd:

Listing 12-2

```
1   # limit the number of sub-processes (using the built-in metric)
2   - metrics.symfony.processes.count < 10
3
4   # be sure we don't hit the cache more than needed
5   - metrics.parses.count == metrics.cache_driver.count
```

You can also limit the number of SQL queries:

Listing 12-3

```
1   - metrics.sql.queries.count < 10
```

What is the ideal number? 5? 10? It really depends on your project. As you know, the fastest code is the code that is never called. Checking that a function is never called is also a very good practice.

Websites with a lot of traffic might want no SQL queries on their homepage:

Listing 12-4

```
1   - metrics.sql.queries.count == 0
```

Another best practice for any website is to never send emails synchronously:

Listing 12-5

```
1   - metrics.emails.sent.count == 0
```

Some more examples on popular PHP libraries:

Listing 12-6

```
1    # check that the Twig C extension is installed
2    - metrics.twig.attributes.php.get.count == 0
3
4    # limit the number of DB connections
5    # can be 2 if you have a specific connection for the session
6    - metrics.sql.connections.count <= 1
7
8    # same for Redis and AMQP
9    - metrics.redis.connections.count <= 1
10   - metrics.amqp.connections.count <= 1
```

Another good practice for production servers is to generate all cached files before a deployment goes live. The following assertions check this assumption:

Listing 12-7

```
1    # no Twig/Smarty compilation
2    - is_dev() or metrics.twig.compile.count == 0
3    - is_dev() or metrics.smarty.compile.count == 0
4
5    # no Symfony metadata checks
6    - is_dev() or metrics.symfony.config_check.count == 0
7
8    # no Doctrine parsing
9    - is_dev() or (metrics.doctrine.annotations.parsed.count +
10   metrics.doctrine.annotations.read.count + metrics.doctrine.dql.parsed.count +
11   metrics.doctrine.entities.metadata.count +
12   metrics.doctrine.proxies.generated.count) == 0
13
```

```
14   # no YAML loaded
15   - is_dev() or metrics.symfony.yaml.reads.count == 0

     # Assetic controller must not be called (assets should be dumped)
     - is_dev() or metrics.assetic.controller.calls.count == 0
```

The is_dev() function returns false when the assertion is run in an environment configured for production usage.

 Are you sure that your last Code Change works?

Back in 2016, I decided to install the Twig C extension on *symfony.com*[1] servers. It took me less than 5 minutes. For good measure, I added the twig.attributes.count == 0 assertion in my Blackfire tests and run a profile... it failed. I double-checked, and I forgot to symlink the new twig.ini configuration I created to the PHP-FPM directory. Easy enough to fix.

But the assertion kept failing. I forgot that at the same time, I also changed the cache directory for Twig templates and PHP was still using the old directory. Again, easy enough to fix.

It took me two or three attempts before I got a green tick from Blackfire. Without Blackfire, I would never have noticed that the C extension was installed but not enabled properly.

Blackfire promotes a metrics-first approach to performance. Write good assertions and they will catch problems before you ever need to analyze a call graph.

Don't be afraid to create custom metrics. This is where Blackfire shines. The ability to create custom assertions based on your team's code patterns is a powerful tool. Reusing a custom metric on an Open-Source library often? Contact us and we will consider adding it to our built-in repository of metrics.

Performance Recommendations

Writing tests is hard as it requires you to find the relevant and actionable metric and to know what is an acceptable value for that metric. But for common frameworks and PHP itself, Blackfire gives you a head start via recommendations!

Performance recommendations are "default" tests that are always run. These tests were written by PHP experts. Anytime you profile your application, if one of those tests fails, you will be warned directly on the profile view. Besides recommendations on PHP itself, Blackfire has solid recommendations for major projects like Symfony, Magento, Drupal, eZPlatform and Typo 3.

---

1. https://symfony.com/

Each recommendation comes with a documentation page that explains why it was written, and how you can fix the issue. If you believe that some recommendations are false positives or not applicable, you can always discard them.

Blackfire goes one step further as recommendations are not just for performance. We worked on a set of quality and security best practices, which we implemented as default tests as well.

Quality recommendations aim specifically at making sure that your are pushing the right configuration in production, for instance that your `php.ini` file and the cache settings are optimized.

Security recommendations help you make sure that you don't push un-secure code or configuration to production. For instance, Blackfire checks if your dependencies have know security vulnerabilities. Most tools that check security issues require you to push some code, but what about that live website which has been running for months with no changes? Check chapter 16 to see how to let Blackfire run automatically and let you know!

 We are very open to improving recommendations, or adding more of them. If you have an expertise that you would like to share, don't hesitate to reach out to us!

Conclusion

Time makes it easier to find the root cause of a performance issue, but it is a poor metric when it comes to performance assertions.

Having the appropriate metrics makes it possible to capture a lot of information about your code, PHP, or any framework you might rely on. And the possibilities are then huge.

Have you realized that most of the assertion examples are related to code behavior rather than performance? Blackfire is not just about performance. Blackfire can be used in an unexpected way: understanding how code works at runtime. This is a fascinating usage, which we will study in the next chapter.

Chapter 13
Understanding Code Behavior

Have you ever dreamed of being a fly on the wall when PHP runs your code and see which functions are executed? Debuggers deliver this experience, but only on development machines. What about production? Blackfire provides a simple and low-overhead tool to understand code behavior at runtime in all environments, including production.

Like any developer, you have already experienced the frustration of trying to understand how a legacy project works. Even on your very own projects, complexity added over the years can make any change difficult. Sometimes you can't even tell if some parts of the code are still used anymore.

The performance optimizations we made on GitList and PHP Mess Detector were quick to find because we had the right tool. Remember that these are popular Open-Source projects and that people read this code and fix bugs all the time... but nobody ever spotted our simple improvements. Blackfire was key to our success.

Want more real-life examples?

What does Composer do When Running an Update?

Have you ever wondered why it takes so long for a "simple" `composer update` to complete? Is it because of the dependency resolution process? Or the package downloads? Does the cache make any difference? Those questions can be easily answered with Blackfire.

In an empty directory, create a Composer file with a dependency on Twig:

Listing 13-1
```
1  {
2      "require": {
3          "twig/twig": "1.20.0"
4      }
5  }
```

Before running Composer, this version of Twig was already cached by Composer and its metadata cache was fully warmed as Composer was just run on another project.

Let's profile the first Composer update:

Listing 13-2

```
1  blackfire run composer up
```

Blackfire generates a profile with *4 HTTP requests*[1].

Profile again and the second time, the profile only contains *3 HTTP requests*[2].

The first time, the **vendor/** directory was empty and Composer installed Twig. Looking at the parent node of the additional **file_get_contents()** call tells us that Composer notified Packagist of this installation, which generated a request to **https://packagist.org/downloads/**:

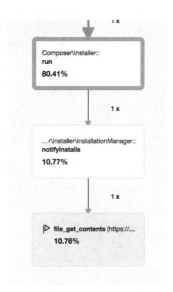

The second time, the call did not happen as Twig was already installed in the correct version in the **vendor/** directory. This is how Packagist counts the number of package installations.

The profiles also reveal that more than half of the wall time is spent downloading files from Packagist, even when there is nothing to do. Take a closer look at these HTTP requests. Notice that the content of the **https://packagist.org/packages.json** URL is always retrieved? This gives Composer all the information it needs to potentially download other files:

Listing 13-3

---

1. https://blackfire.io/profiles/1e57728f-dd0b-4b2a-b076-c1c98f6d9023/graph
2. https://blackfire.io/profiles/9b6e4413-2028-4d28-bc2f-60c9263136b6/graph

```
 1  {
 2      "notify": "/downloads/%package%",
 3      "notify-batch": "/downloads/",
 4      "packages": [],
 5      "provider-includes": {
 6          "p/provider-2013$%hash%.json": {
 7              "sha256":
 8  "5eabcb75d94b428ce510270878b2b10a81e00b8afaaf4d5e9896b274ec0fbeaa"
 9          },
10          "p/provider-2014$%hash%.json": {
11              "sha256":
12  "9a7a79cfdfd24dac773cf189faa0a6756b33f4352c39e7861ed55cb870e27b32"
13          },
14          "p/provider-2015-01$%hash%.json": {
15              "sha256":
16  "00340913136e82907716efe89d8980d7d3e47b390905f6d72f0ff56eebb9cb66"
17          },
18          "p/provider-2015-04$%hash%.json": {
19              "sha256":
20  "dc1d338b4e059389de2091992417eff634f94835ecb96498aa2259bfabffbc25"
21          },
22          "p/provider-2015-07$%hash%.json": {
23              "sha256":
24  "99a9efb2c3970745412fdef4b55438a77afae24b84e95fa552a2dfcca21495c1"
25          },
26          "p/provider-2015-10$%hash%.json": {
27              "sha256":
28  "113e6db06a47bbe901f6932307011daf9de612ca9de927cd2ff263a34b234263"
29          },
30          "p/provider-archived$%hash%.json": {
31              "sha256":
32  "21bb16829b6e507a79cf2a99773416f62462506f86d2f8a04167454724e08946"
33          },
           "p/provider-latest$%hash%.json": {
               "sha256":
       "29734ba3922c24ce8eb0f9bdfe765b2a4ed346e8e399c9d59c8faf57af2afb03"
           }
       },
       "providers-url": "/p/%package%$%hash%.json",
       "search": "/search.json?q=%query%"
   }
```

Take some time to analyze the call graph and the function calls, you will learn a lot about how Composer works.

 Running Composer with the **-vvv** flag displays many logs about what Composer is doing. This is quite entertaining while waiting for the command to complete.

What is the Difference Between Symfony Development and Production Environments?

The Symfony full-stack framework provides an environment feature that lets developers tweak their project configuration for development, test, or production environments. In the "dev" environment for instance, logs are verbose, caches are disabled, and auto-reload of configuration and Twig templates is enabled. That adds some significant overhead. Can we watch the different code paths with Blackfire?

As an example, I have profiled the symfony.com website homepage in the development environment and in the production environment on my local machine.

To better understand the difference between the environments, compare the two profiles. The comparison makes it very clear that the Symfony production environment is much faster and consumes less memory than its development counterpart:

The comparison call graph reveals that some additional function calls are responsible for the slow-down in the "dev" environment:

- The event dispatcher is wrapped by an instance of `TraceableEventDispatcher`, which records various metrics about triggered events:

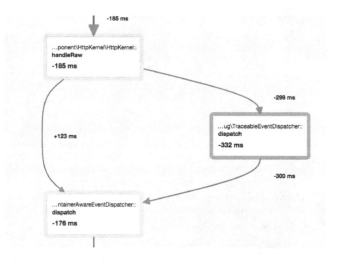

It works by wrapping all listeners:

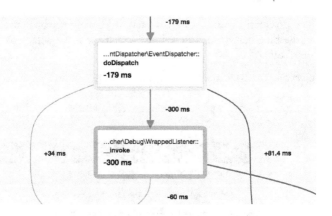

- The Twig engine is also wrapped by `TwigTimedEngine` again to gather information about rendered templates:

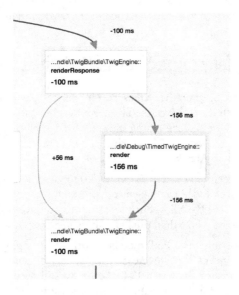

The function calls table also gives more hints about the differences:

- The autoloader used in development, `DebugClassLoader`, is different from the one used in production, `ApcClassLoader`:

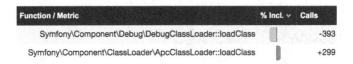

Function / Metric	% Incl. ⌄	Calls
Symfony\Component\Debug\DebugClassLoader::loadClass		-393
Symfony\Component\ClassLoader\ApcClassLoader::loadClass		+299

The production autoloader is faster, as you can see by comparing the size of the blue bar versus the red one (open the node details to confirm with numbers).

Sort the function calls table by the number of calls, and again, learn more:

- Monolog is way more verbose in development than it is in production:

Function / Metric	% Incl.	Calls ⌄
Monolog\Formatter\NormalizerFormatter::normalize@1		-2 100
Monolog\Formatter\LineFormatter::stringify		-1 800
Monolog\Formatter\LineFormatter::convertToString		-1 800

In less than 5 minutes, we learned a lot about Symfony internals without having to look at its code. If you want to learn more about what these classes do, it is now a matter of reading the source code of the corresponding classes.

Why is Symfony's `ApacheUrlMatcher` Slow?

In an attempt to speed up the request routing process, Symfony 2.0 was released with an `ApacheUrlMatcher` class. The basic responsibility of this class was to generate a block of Apache configuration with a bunch of `mod_rewrite` rules. The goal was to make the URL matching process much faster by delegating the bulk of the work to Apache.

This class has been removed in Symfony 3.0 for several reasons: the first one is that some features added to the Symfony Routing components were not easy to convert to `mod_rewrite` rules, but more importantly, we realized that this class actually performed worse than the PHP implementation.

How is that possible? The PHP matcher works by dumping an optimized PHP file so that we never have to create the expensive route collection object at runtime. When using the `ApacheUrlMatcher` we still needed to create the route collection object for every request. So, even though the seemingly time-consuming matching process was already done by Apache, the process as a whole ended up taking much longer than expected.

The interesting part of this story is that it took us years to find this issue, and the process of debugging the root cause of the slow down was quite tricky. Blackfire could have shown us the problem right away.

Conclusion

Blackfire profiles can help understand which parts of your codebase are executed. Profile comparisons help understand code behavior differences. Try using Blackfire on your own projects, not to find performance bottlenecks, but just to get a new perspective on your code. You might discover behaviors you would not have expected.

Chapter 14

Profiling Consumers

Blackfire can be used to profile anything PHP, from incoming HTTP requests to executed CLI scripts, but what about consumers and daemons? Relying on Blackfire's auto-instrumentation for consumers and daemons is impossible, since they run for a very long period of time. If a script never ends, the profile will never be complete and will never show up on Blackfire.

In the PHP world, long running scripts are mostly consumers: they consume messages from a queue or read messages from a database.

Profiling a consumer commonly consists of instrumenting the code executed in the main loop. There are many possible profiling strategies, depending on what your consumer does and the kinds of messages it deals with.

Never-ending PHP Consumers as Daemons

Consumers written in PHP can be written with the following:

Listing 14-1
```
1   // create an infinite loop
2   for (;;) {
3       // do something
4   }
```

The above code runs indefinitely **in the foreground**. To make it a "real" daemon and run your PHP consumer in the background, use standard Unix tools like Upstart.

Installing the PHP SDK

The Blackfire PHP SDK provides a nice API that, amongst other things, gives you access to the Blackfire PHP instrumentation triggering system.

All you need to get started is to install the SDK via Composer:

Listing 14-2

```
1   composer require blackfire/php-sdk
```

 Do not add Blackfire's SDK as a dev dependency (**--dev**) as code relying on it should work in production as well.

Using the PHP SDK

Create a `consumer.php` file with the following content:

Listing 14-3
```
1   require_once __DIR__.'/vendor/autoload.php';
2
3   use Blackfire\Client;
4
5   function consume()
6   {
7       echo "Message consumed!\n";
8   }
9
10  $blackfire = new Client();
11
12  $probe = $blackfire->createProbe();
13
14  consume();
15
16  $profile = $blackfire->endProbe($probe);
17
18  print $profile->getUrl()."\n";
```

Run it like any regular PHP script:

Listing 14-4
```
1   php consumer.php
```

The `Blackfire\Client` instance created on line 10 is the main SDK entry point. To profile a piece of code, wrap it with `createProbe()` (line 12) and `endProbe()` (line 16). Line 18 displays the URL where you can access the generated profile.

Some major differences between auto-instrumentation and using the SDK:

- The SDK allows you to create several profiles from one script execution (create several probes);
- The SDK returns the profile as an object, giving you the opportunity to get profiling data right in the script (which you might use to make decisions);
- The SDK gathers less information as it hooks into the PHP engine much later and leaves much sooner than when auto-instrumentation is used (even if `createProbe()` and `endProbe()` are the very first and the very last line of the script);
- To run the script, **do not** use `blackfire run` as instrumentation and profile generation is triggered directly from the code itself (the Blackfire command line tool main responsibility is to generate a signature, which is done when calling the PHP SDK `createProbe()` method).

Instrumenting a Consumer

A naive implementation of a consumer might profile all consumed messages:

Listing 14-5

```
1   $blackfire = new Client();
2
3   for (;;) {
4       $probe = $blackfire->createProbe();
5
6       consume();
7
8       $profile = $blackfire->endProbe($probe);
9
10      print $profile->getUrl()."\n";
11
12      usleep(10000);
13  }
```

This implementation suffers from several problems:

- On busy consumers, this code will generate tons of profiles that nobody will ever look at;
- The code is not optimal as all message consumptions are affected by Blackfire's overhead;
- Each profile leads to several HTTP round-trips to Blackfire's servers, slowing down the consumer significantly;
- Profiles that aggregate several iterations of the same code might be more accurate.

If all consumed messages are of the same type you can use the PHP SDK to aggregate several messages into one profile:

Listing 14-6

```
1   require_once __DIR__.'/vendor/autoload.php';
2
3   use Blackfire\Client;
4   use Blackfire\Profile\Configuration as ProfileConfiguration;
5
6   function consume()
7   {
8       echo "Message consumed!\n";
9   }
10
11  $blackfire = new Client();
12  $maxIterations = 10;
13  $currentIteration = 0;
14  $profileConfig = new ProfileConfiguration();
15  $profileConfig->setTitle('Consumer')->setSamples($maxIterations);
16
17  for (;;) {
18      if (0 === $currentIteration) {
19          $probe = $blackfire->createProbe($profileConfig, false);
20      }
21
22      $probe->enable();
23
24      consume();
25
26      $probe->close();
```

```
27
28      ++$currentIteration;
29      if ($currentIteration === $maxIterations) {
30          $profile = $blackfire->endProbe($probe);
31          $currentIteration = 0;
32
33          print $profile->getUrl()."\n";
34      }
35
36      usleep(10000);
37  }
```

There is a lot going on here. Let's describe the code in more detail:

- Line 14: Create a Blackfire\Profile\Configuration instance that holds profile configuration: the number of iterations for each profile (10) and the profile title (Consumer);
- Lines 18-20: The probe does not exist yet or a profile has just been generated in the previous iteration, create a new profile (false disables probe auto-start);
- Line 22: Starts a new iteration for the current profile;
- Line 26: Stops the iteration;
- Line 31-33: The max iterations is reached, end the profile and send the data back to Blackfire.

The output should look like the following:

Listing 14-7

```
1   Message consumed!
2   Message consumed!
3   Message consumed!
4   Message consumed!
5   Message consumed!
6   Message consumed!
7   Message consumed!
8   Message consumed!
9   Message consumed!
10  Message consumed!
11  https://blackfire.io/profiles/602e1a37-b7e4-46d5-838c-ac8da38d9006/graph
12  Message consumed!
13  Message consumed!
14  Message consumed!
15  Message consumed!
16  Message consumed!
17  Message consumed!
18  Message consumed!
19  Message consumed!
20  Message consumed!
21  Message consumed!
22  https://blackfire.io/profiles/a027fb95-2c03-470f-8184-e9af6a1cdd14/graph
```

This is better but not perfect, as we are still profiling all messages. What about profiling only some messages? Like 1% of all messages, or 10 messages every hour?

As an exercise, modify the code to generate a profile of 10 messages in a row every 1,000 messages.

If the Blackfire C extension is not available on all your machines, make the Blackfire code conditional with the following condition:

Listing 14-8

```
1   if (extension_loaded('blackfire')) {
2       // do something related to Blackfire
3   }
```

Using the PHP's SDK LoopClient

The last example contains a lot of boilerplate code that can be avoided by using Blackfire's LoopClient class:

Listing 14-9

```
1   require_once __DIR__.'/vendor/autoload.php';
2
3   use Blackfire\LoopClient;
4   use Blackfire\Client;
5   use Blackfire\Profile\Configuration as ProfileConfiguration;
6
7   function consume()
8   {
9       echo "Message consumed!\n";
10  }
11
12  $blackfire = new LoopClient(new Client(), 10);
13  $profileConfig = new ProfileConfiguration();
14  $profileConfig->setTitle('Consumer');
15
16  for (;;) {
17      $blackfire->startLoop($profileConfig);
18
19      consume();
20
21      if ($profile = $blackfire->endLoop()) {
22          print $profile->getUrl()."\n";
23      }
24
25      usleep(400000);
26  }
```

The LoopClient constructor takes a Blackfire Client instance and the number of iterations for each profile. The startLoop() and endLoop() methods have the same logic as the code from before.

Profiling a consumer continuously is probably never a good idea. Instead, trigger profiles from the outside using signals.

Conclusion

Most PHP users fear consumers written in PHP as they are seen as convoluted black boxes. Not anymore. With Blackfire's PHP SDK and only a few small changes, you can now better understand your consumers and probably optimize them.

The ability to manually instrument code with the Blackfire PHP SDK opens up a lot of opportunities. One of them is the integration of Blackfire in your unit test suite, which is our next topic.

Chapter 15

Integrating with Unit Tests

Unit tests rarely come to mind when talking about performance management. This is for a good reason: tests depending on time lead to transient failures. Blackfire lets developers write tests on stable metrics that are related to the root causes of performance issues instead of time. Using such metrics in a unit test suite is a powerful option.

To make things more concrete, let's write some unit tests for the Gitter `Gitter\Client::getVersion()` method we optimized previously. The test suite already has a test covering the output of the method:

Listing 15-1

```
1   public function testIsParsingGitVersion()
2   {
3       $version = $this->client->getVersion();
4       $this->assertNotEmpty($version);
5   }
```

But how can we test that `git --version` only runs the very first time `getVersion()` is called? Have a look at the `getVersion()` method implementation and note the usage of the `Process` class:

Listing 15-2

```
1   public function getVersion()
2   {
3       static $version;
4
5       if (null !== $version) {
6           return $version;
7       }
8
9       $process = new Process($this->getPath() . ' --version');
10      $process->run();
11
12      if (!$process->isSuccessful()) {
13          throw new \RuntimeException($process->getErrorOutput());
14      }
15
16      $version = trim(substr($process->getOutput(), 12));
17      return $version;
18  }
```

As PHPUnit cannot mock the **Process** instance, we need to find another way:

- We can re-define the Process class (extending the real one and wrapping the start() method) before running any tests and register it before Composer's autoloader kicks in. That's rather ugly, fragile, and confusing to do it by hand but some mocking libraries can help you achieve that.
- Use Blackfire!

Using Blackfire in PHPUnit

Let's see how Blackfire integrates with PHPUnit. The easiest way is to include the **Blackfire\Bridge\Phpunit\TestCaseTrait** trait.

Listing 15-3

```
1  use Blackfire\Bridge\Phpunit\TestCaseTrait as BlackfireTrait;
2  use PHPUnit\Framework\TestCase;
3
4  class ClientTest extends TestCase
5  {
6      use BlackfireTrait;
7  }
```

Trait support was added in PHP 5.4. For older PHP versions, read the PHPUnit integration documentation for a workaround.

Then, create a PHPUnit test like this one:

Listing 15-4

```
1   use Blackfire\Profile\Configuration as ProfileConfiguration;
2
3   public function testIsGitVersionCached()
4   {
5       $config = new ProfileConfiguration();
6       $config->assert('metrics.symfony.processes.count == 1', 'One Process call
7   only');
8
9       $this->assertBlackfire($config, function () {
10          $this->client->getVersion();
11          $this->client->getVersion();
12          $this->client->getVersion();
13      });
    }
```

The **assertBlackfire()** call is where the magic happens:

- It takes a configuration where some Blackfire assertions are defined (metrics.symfony.processes.count == 1);
- It instruments the code in the anonymous function before running it;
- It converts the Blackfire assertions to PHPUnit ones so that errors and failures are injected into PHPUnit's report, as any other assertion.

Be sure to add this test **before** any other tests; if not, the cache could be already warmed and the test would fail. To make the test more robust, move the $version variable as a static class variable and use reflection to reset its state at the beginning of the test:

Listing 15-5

```
1  $p = new \ReflectionProperty($this->client, 'version');
2  $p->setAccessible(true);
3
4  $p->setValue($this->client, null);
```

Debugging Failures and Errors

If the test fails, PHPUnit displays a nice error message with all the information you need to debug it:

Listing 15-6

```
1  F
2
3  Time: 3.03 seconds, Memory: 15.00Mb
4
5  There was 1 failure:
6
7  1) Gitter\Tests\ClientTest::testIsGitVersionCached
8  Failed asserting that Blackfire tests pass.
9  1 tests failures out of 1.
10
11     failed: One Process only
12       - metrics.process.count 3 == 1
13
14  More information at https://blackfire.io/profiles/
15  4427f830-62fe-469f-b6aa-8ad8f6dcdff7/graph.
16
17  /.../gitter/vendor/blackfire/php-sdk/src/Blackfire/Bridge/PhpUnit/
18  TestConstraint.php:60
19  /.../gitter/vendor/blackfire/php-sdk/src/Blackfire/Bridge/Phpunit/
20  TestCaseTrait.php:48
21  /.../gitter/tests/Gitter/Tests/ClientTest.php:60

   FAILURES!
   Tests: 1, Assertions: 1, Failures: 1.
```

If cache is commented out, the assertion fails as 3 processes are run. The call graph URL points to the profile where you can debug problems more easily.

If the assertion has a syntax error, the profile "Assertions" tab helps you understand the problem:

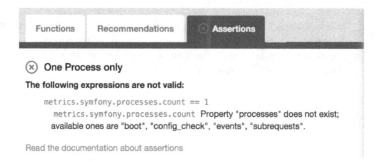

The following expressions are not valid:

```
metrics.symfony.processes.count == 1
    metrics.symfony.processes.count Property "processes" does not exist;
    available ones are "boot", "config_check", "events", "subrequests".
```

Read the documentation about assertions

Defining your own Metrics

This test was easy to write because we were able to use a built-in metric, but this is not always the case. Luckily, it is possible to create custom metrics with the PHP SDK:

Listing 15-7
```
1  use Blackfire\Profile\Configuration as ProfileConfiguration;
2  use Blackfire\Profile\Metric;
3
4  $config = new ProfileConfiguration();
5
6  $config->defineMetric(new Metric('process', '=Symfony\Component\Process\
7  Process::start'));
   $config->assert('metrics.process.count == 1', 'One Process only');
```

Conclusion

Read our PHPUnit integration documentation for more tips on how to leverage Blackfire in PHPUnit test suites.

Blackfire lets you test your code's behavior without the need for mocks. This is a very useful technique when you need to test the behavior of a third-party library you cannot easily modify. With Blackfire there is no need to change third-party code or write an ugly hack. Simple define custom metrics and write assertions against them.

Using Blackfire in a PHPUnit test has one great side-effect: your performance tests automatically benefit from your continuous integration setup. Automation is key for continuously managing performance, and this is the topic for the next few chapters.

Chapter 16

Performance Automation

Do you know why most developers don't manage the performance of their applications? Many will tell you they don't have the time, but the real reason is probably that they don't have the right tools. Blackfire fills this gap. Being able to profile applications in development and diagnose problems in production is great, but if the process is manual, developers will stop doing it after a while.

Automation is key to continuously manage application performance.

Automation is also key to avoid performance regressions in production. Blackfire provides a feature that helps developers trigger performance tests on an application and be alerted whenever a problem occurs.

Writing Scenarios

Manually triggering profiles on individual URLs like we did previously works well on development machines, but it does not scale well for production monitoring.

Blackfire scenarios let you run a set of profiles on your application's main URLs or API endpoints. Scenarios are defined in **.blackfire.yml** under the **scenarios** section.

GitList scenarios could look like the following:

Listing 16-1

```
1   scenarios:
2       Homepage:
3           - /
4       Twig Homepage:
5           - /Twig
6       Twig Commits:
7           - /Twig/commits
8       Twig Stats:
9           - /Twig/stats
10      Twig Network:
11          - /Twig/network
12      Twig Network Ajax
```

```
13           - /Twig/network/1.x
14       Search:
15           - /Twig
16           - path: /Twig/tree/1.x/search?query=loader
17             method: POST
18             samples: 10
19             warmup: true
```

Each scenario has a name and a list of URLs to profile; but only the last URL of each scenario is profiled.

In the example, all scenarios, but the last one, trigger profiles on HTTP GET requests. For each one of them, Blackfire warms up the URL by hitting it a few times before generating a profile out of several iterations.

The "Search" scenario is more interesting as it requests a POST request, but a safe one. By default, scenarios for non-GET requests have no warmup and profiles are generated from only one iteration. But as GitList search is *idempotent*, the scenario is explicitly configured to enable warmup (warmup: true) and to generate 10 requests (samples: 10) for the profile.

 Blackfire scenarios have more options as described in the scenarios documentation.

Triggering Scenarios

Now that the GitList scenarios are defined, we need a way to trigger them. Blackfire has several ways to trigger them, but the most simple one is to use a **periodic build**.

Periodic Builds

Select your Environment, go to the Builds tab and click the "Enable periodic builds" button. By default, Blackfire will launch a new build every 6 hours. But you can fine-tune those settings. Click on the "Edit" icon.

By default, Blackfire will run builds on the endpoint you define when you created the environment, but you can change that. However, periodic builds can target a single endpoint. You'll need to create multiple environments if you want to periodic run builds on multiple endpoints.

Webhook

 The Enterprise Edition of Blackfire offers all ways to trigger them, such as the webhook.

Go to the Dashboard's **Builds** tab of your environment and click the "Start a build" button:

Then enter the endpoint (`https://gitlist.demo.blackfire.io/`), trigger the build by submitting the form, and wait for the profiles to finish.

Alternatively, you can also copy and paste the generated URL at the bottom of the form in a console:

Listing 16-2

```
1  curl -i -X POST https://blackfire.io/api/v1/build/env/__UUID__/webhook \
2  --user '$user_id:$user_token' \
3  -d 'endpoint=https://gitlist.demo.blackfire.io/' \
4  -d 'title=My First Scenario!'
```

To use the command above, replace the __UUID__ placeholder with the UUID of one of your Blackfire environments.

If the trigger fired correctly, the JSON output should contain "A new build has been started". Go to the Blackfire dashboard, then to the "Builds" tab and select the newest build:

Build Report

With one simple request, we were able to automatically generate 7 profiles in parallel for the main GitList URLs.

The build report displays all profile results, highlights failed scenarios, and provides details for any failed assertions:

As expected, some scenarios fail. Next execute the scenarios on the **fix2** branch (from the web or from the console), where our performance patches have been applied:

```
1  curl -i -X POST https://blackfire.io/api/v1/build/env/__UUID__/webhook \
2  --user '$user_id:$user_token' \
3  -d 'endpoint=https://fix2-ijtxpsladv67o.eu.platform.sh/' \
4  -d 'title=Scenario on the fix2 branch'
```

The results are definitely better, but not as good as we could have hoped. Have a closer look and you will realize that some pages are slower than expected. This is the time to dig into the root causes and try to find more optimizations.

 Remember that the main benefits of storing scenarios in a `.blackfire.yml` file alongside your code is to make them specific to your current work: a pull request, a branch, a specific version of your code, etc. Whenever you add a new feature, don't forget to update the scenarios.

Being Notified

Webhooks are a great way to integrate Blackfire into any tool. Then, once your checks are automated, you will need a way to be alerted when performance degrades.

Blackfire notification channels alert you when a build fails or when a project's status changes. Blackfire comes with many built-in notification channels, but the simplest one is the **email notification channel**.

On the dashboard Builds view, add an email notification channel. Configure the email notification channel to receive an email whenever there is a failure or when the build status changes:

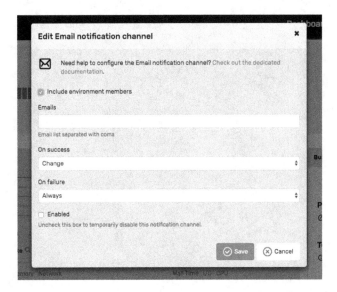

Conclusion

In development, update your application scenarios whenever you make significant changes.

Configure your test environment to run the scenarios via the webhook and use the email notification channel to receive a notification whenever a build fails.

For production, configure the Blackfire "Periodic builds" to automatically profile your application on a periodic basis and use the Slack, Hipchat or Microsoft Teams notification channel to get fast feedback.

But there is more. Builds are also available in the PHP SDK, which opens the door to dynamically building scenarios. The SDK is the best way to leverage Blackfire powerful features, and in the next chapter we will study some advanced usages.

Chapter 17

Doing more with the SDK

The PHP SDK allows to programmatically control Blackfire. We have already covered how to leverage the SDK in unit tests and how to use the SDK to profile consumers and daemons in previous chapters. This chapter outlines several advanced usages of the PHP SDK. Hopefully these examples will inspire you to create your own implementations. Your imagination is really the only limit here.

Monitoring Consumers Performance

In a previous chapter, we used the `LoopClient` class to instrument consumers:

Listing 17-1

```
1  for (;;) {
2      $blackfire->startLoop($profileConfig);
3
4      consume();
5
6      $blackfire->endLoop();
7
8      usleep(400000);
9  }
```

If you read the documentation about how to profile consumers, you should be familiar with using signals to instrument your production code. It works like this:

Listing 17-2

```
1  use Blackfire\LoopClient;
2
3  $blackfire = new LoopClient(new Client(), 10);
4  $blackfire->setSignal(SIGUSR1);
5  $blackfire->attachReference(7);
6  $blackfire->promoteReferenceSignal(SIGUSR2);
```

- When you start the consumer process, it behaves as usual with **no overhead**: Blackfire does not instrument the code and the calls to startLoop() and endLoop() are effectively no-ops. This is **perfect for production**.

- When the process receives the configured signal (SIGUSR1 in the example), Blackfire instruments the code for the next 10 iterations (as configured above), generates a profile, and disables instrumentation again.

  When Blackfire's servers receive the profile, associated **tests are run**.

  The generated profiles will also be automatically linked to the reference (7) and **comparison tests are run** as well.

- When signaling the process with SIGUSR2, a profile is generated like with the main signal, but the new profile becomes the new reference profile.

  Signal the consumer with SIGUSR2 whenever you **deploy a new version of the code**. Add it as a step in your deployment script and get consumer profiling automation for free.

Whenever you want to better understand the status of one of your consumers, signal it once and be done. That gives you on-demand profiles, but how can you achieve scheduled builds for consumers? As you might have guessed, this is a matter of configuring a cron job:

Listing 17.3

```
1  # generate a profile every hour
2  0 * * * * pkill -SIGUSR1 -f consumer.php
```

If you want to be notified whenever some tests fail, create builds and configure a notification channel to receive build statuses and reports.

The PHP SDK provides everything you need to start builds programmatically (see below), but LoopClient makes it even easier. Call generateBuilds() and pass it the environment name or UUID:

Listing 17.4

```
1  $blackfire->generateBuilds('ENV_NAME_OR_UUID');
```

And you have it: **a fully automated way to continuously profile consumers**, monitor their intrinsic performance, and their performance evolution over time.

Instrumenting Code Manually

When using the Companion or the Blackfire CLI tool to trigger a profile, there is no need to change the code. Blackfire takes care of everything for you. But what if you want to profile only part of the executed code? That's possible by explicitly marking the code you want to profile.

 Do not confuse using the PHP SDK to **manually create profiles** (which does not need the Companion or the CLI tool) with manually instrumenting the code with the SDK, which helps Blackfire generate precise profiles when triggered by the Companion or CLI tool.

First, retrieve the current probe:

Listing 17-5

```
1   // Get the probe main instance
2   $probe = \BlackfireProbe::getMainInstance();
```

Then, call **enable()** to start the profiling and **disable()** to stop it:

Listing 17-6

```
1   // start profiling the code
2   $probe->enable();
3
4   // code that you want to profile
5
6   // stop the profiling
7   $probe->disable();
```

You do not need to install the Blackfire SDK to benefit from this feature as the **BlackfireProbe** class is part of the Blackfire C extension.

You can mark as many sections as you want, but be warned that all sections are going to be part of the same call graph. Including too many unrelated sections will generate a convoluted, useless profile.

As soon as you explicitly call **enable()** in your code, Blackfire understands that you want to control what to instrument and disables auto-instrumentation.

As with auto-instrumentation, profiling is only active when the code is run through the Companion or the Blackfire CLI utility. If a profile has not been triggered, calls to the probe are just ignored.

Profiling HTTP Controllers

Web frameworks provide a common abstraction to handle HTTP requests that can be quite noisy on a call graph. When debugging a performance issue, you might want to focus on the executed controller code only. Using manual instrumentation can be useful; here is an example of a PSR-7 middleware that you can use with *Zend Expressive*[1]:

```
1   use Psr\Http\Message\ResponseInterface;
2   use Psr\Http\Message\ServerRequestInterface;
3   use Zend\Stratigility\MiddlewareInterface;
4
5   class BlackfireMiddleware implements MiddlewareInterface
6   {
7       public function __invoke(ServerRequestInterface $request,
8   ResponseInterface $response, callable $out = null)
9       {
10          $probe = null;
11          if (class_exists('BlackfireProbe', false)) {
12              $probe = BlackfireProbe::getMainInstance();
13          }
14
15          if (null !== $out) {
16              $probe and $probe->enable();
17              $response = $out($request, $response);
18              $probe and $probe->close();
19          }
20
21          return $response;
22      }
   }
```

Listing 17-7

Profiling ReactPHP Servers

The same technique can be used to profile HTTP requests handled by PHP servers like *ReactPHP*[2]. Blackfire's PHP SDK provides a helper class to ease the integration, which is detailed in this blog post.

Instrumenting Outgoing API Calls

Some projects consist of a set of micro-services written in PHP, all communicating via HTTP. When profiling a user-facing HTTP request for such a project, the call graph contains many HTTP calls for which Blackfire only displays the URL and the wall time. If one of the requests is slow, you need to manually trigger another profile against that microservice in order to understand the bottlenecks.

---

1. https://github.com/zendframework/zend-expressive
2. https://reactphp.org/

Wouldn't it be great if you could automatically generate profiles for these API calls? The implementation depends on the HTTP library you are using to make your API calls, but the general idea looks like this:

Listing 17-8

```
1  $probe = \BlackfireProbe::getMainInstance();
2
3  if ($probe->getResponseLine()) {
4      $client = new \Blackfire\Client();
5
6      $request = $client->createRequest();
7      $header = 'X-Blackfire-Query: '.$request->getToken();
8
9      // add the header to the external HTTP request call
10 }
```

- *Line 1*: Get the probe for the current HTTP request;
- *Line 3*: Make sure that a profile was actually requested - if not, there is nothing to do;
- *Line 6*: Create a new profile request;
- *Line 7*: Generate an HTTP header containing the signature needed to trigger a new profile;
- *Line 9*: Finally, add this header to the outgoing request to trigger an additional profile for the sub-request.

If you are using Guzzle, you can simplify the code as Blackfire provides a native integration:

Listing 17-9

```
1  $options = array();
2
3  $probe = \BlackfireProbe::getMainInstance();
4  if ($probe->getResponseLine()) {
5      $options['blackfire'] = true;
6  }
7
8  $response = $guzzle->request('GET', $url, $options);
```

You can find more information about profiling HTTP requests with the PHP SDK in the documentation.

Generating Builds Programmatically

Creating builds via the SDK is another very powerful feature, which looks like this:

Listing 17-10

```
1  // create a build
2  $build = $blackfire->startBuild('example_env', array('title' => 'Build from PHP'));
3
4  // create a scenario
5  $scenario = $blackfire->startScenario($build, array('title' => 'My first
6  scenario'));
7
8  // add some profiles to the scenario, see below
```

```
 9
10   // end the scenario and fetch the report
11   $report = $blackfire->closeScenario($scenario);
12
13   // end the build
14   $blackfire->closeBuild($build);
15
16   // print the report URL
     print $report->getUrl();
```

Attaching profiles to a build can be done via the profile configuration:

```
1   // create a configuration
2   $config = new \Blackfire\Profile\Configuration();
3
4   // attach the scenario
5   $config->setScenario($scenario);
```

How do you generate profiles now? There are so many ways that it is up to you! Use the SDK to generate profiles for the current executed code:

```
1   // generate a profile via the SDK
2   $probe = $blackfire->createProbe($config);
3
4   // some PHP code you want to profile
5
6   $blackfire->endProbe($probe);
7
8   // generate some other profiles if that makes sense
```

Or use Guzzle for HTTP requests:

```
1   // generate a profile with Guzzle
2   $response = $guzzle->request('GET', $url, array(
3       'blackfire' => $config,
4   ));
```

Conclusion

Blackfire exposes a lot of features through the PHP SDK. This chapter showed you various ways to use the SDK to solve advanced use cases.

The next logical step for the last recipe would be to generate dynamic scenarios and store the results in build, taking flexibility to the next level. This is a great topic for the next chapter.

Chapter 18

Crawling and Scraping HTTP Applications

In the PHP world, crawling web applications can be done via *Guzzle*[1] or by using a web crawler like *Goutte*[2], which adds a nice DOM manipulation layer on top of Guzzle. Functional or acceptance tests for Web applications can be written via some other Open-Source projects like *Behat*[3] or *Codeception*[4].

Blackfire provides an alternative Open-Source tool that sits between the web crawling and functional testing spaces: *Blackfire Player*[5]. This is an exciting tool that lets developers define crawling scenarios, set expectations on responses, and of course run Blackfire assertions against your code. The main advantage of Blackfire Player over existing solutions is the balance it offers between native features and the simplicity of writing custom crawlers.

The easiest way to use Blackfire Player is to download the phar file:

Listing 18-1
```
1  curl -OLsS http://get.blackfire.io/blackfire-player.phar
```

Then, use `php blackfire-player.phar` to run the player or make it executable and move it to a directory in your `PATH`:

Listing 18-2
```
1  chmod 755 blackfire-player.phar
2  mv blackfire-player.phar .../bin/blackfire-player
```

---

1. http://guzzlephp.org
2. https://github.com/FriendsOfPHP/Goutte
3. http://behat.org/
4. https://codeception.com/
5. https://github.com/blackfireio/player

Crawling an HTTP Application

Let's crawl the GitList application by defining a scenario in a **gitlist.bkf** file:

Listing 18-3

```
1   endpoint 'https://gitlist.demo.blackfire.io/'
2
3   name 'GitList Scenarios'
4
5   scenario
6       name 'Check first repository'
7
8       visit url('/')
9           name 'Homepage'
10          expect status_code() == 200
11          expect header('content_type') matches '/html/'
12          expect css('footer').text() matches '/Powered by GitList/'
```

A scenario can have several **steps** (like **visit**, **click** or **submit**), each one having its own options.

With the **visit** step, you must provide a mandatory URL to hit; like **url('/')**.

Other options used in this example are:

- expect: Some optional expectations on the HTTP response.
- name: The step name.

Run the scenario via the **blackfire-player** command line tool:

Listing 18-4

```
1   blackfire-player run gitlist.bkf -vv
```

The **-vv** increases the verbosity of the output and adds some information about the HTTP interactions with the application:

Listing 18-5

```
1   Blackfire Player
2
3   Scenario  "Check first repository"
4     "Homepage"
5   GET https://gitlist.demo.blackfire.io/
6     OK
7
8   OK  Scenarios  1  - Steps  1
```

If an expectation fails, the scenario is stopped and an error message is displayed. The command also exits with a status code of **64** instead of **0**:

Listing 18-6

```
1   Blackfire Player
2
3   Scenario  "Check first repository"
4     "Homepage"
5   GET https://gitlist.demo.blackfire.io/
6     Failure on step  "Homepage"  defined in gitlist.bkf at line  6
7     └ Expectation "css('footer').text() matches '/Powered by PHP/'" failed.
8       └ css("footer").text() = "Powered by GitList 0.5.0
9   "
10
11  KO  Scenarios  1  - Steps  1  - Failures  1
```

Use -vvv to make the logs very verbose. This flag adds debug information to the output.

Running Assertions

In addition to expectations, the player can also generate profiles and run assertions defined in the .blackfire.yml file by passing the --blackfire-env flag (all profiles are stored in a build):

Listing 18-7

```
1  blackfire-player run gitlist.bkf --blackfire-env=ENV_NAME_OR_UUID -vv
```

The output displays failed assertions:

Listing 18-8

```
1   Blackfire Player
2
3   Scenario  "Check first repository"
4    "Homepage"
5   GET https://gitlist.demo.blackfire.io/
6
7     Failure on step  "Homepage"  defined in gitlist.bkf at line  6
8     └ Assertions failed:
9        metrics.twig.display.count + metrics.twig.render.count < 5
10  Blackfire Report at https://blackfire.io/build-sets/
11  2c44ba7d-139b-41ca-b843-a3d1e2763539
12
      KO  Scenarios  1  - Steps  1  - Failures  1
```

Now, override the endpoint to https://fix2-ijtxpsladv67o.eu.platform.sh/ via the --endpoint flag:

Listing 18-9

```
1  blackfire-player run gitlist.bkf \
2  --blackfire-env=ENV_NAME_OR_UUID \
3  --endpoint=https://fix2-ijtxpsladv67o.eu.platform.sh/ \
4  -vv
```

Blackfire assertions should pass and the scenario should end successfully.

By default when using the --blackfire-env option (which is the case when ran from our servers), each step is automatically profiled. To disable Blackfire, use the blackfire setting:

Listing 18-10

```
1  visit url('/')
2     name 'Homepage'
3     blackfire false
```

Clicking on Links

Instead of visiting the Twig project URL, we could also have clicked on the link:

Listing 18-11

```
1  endpoint 'https://gitlist.demo.blackfire.io/'
2
```

```
 3   name 'GitList Scenarios'
 4
 5   scenario
 6       name 'Check first repository'
 7
 8       visit url('/')
 9           name 'Homepage'
10           expect status_code() == 200
11           expect header('content_type') matches '/html/'
12           expect css('footer').text() matches '/Powered by GitList/'
13
14       click link('Twig')
15           name "First Project Page"
16           expect status_code() == 200
17           expect css('.breadcrumb li a').text() matches '/Twig/'
```

The link() function finds a link on the current page based on its name. You can also click on links via CSS selectors:

Listing 18-12
```
 1   click css('.repository a').first()
```

Values Extraction

Now let's rewrite the scenario and remove the hardcoding of Twig by using **variable extraction**:

Listing 18-13
```
 1   visit url('/')
 2       name 'Homepage'
 3       expect status_code() == 200
 4       expect header('content_type') matches '/html/'
 5       expect css('footer').text() matches '/Powered by GitList/'
 6       set repo_name css('.repository a').first().text()
 7
 8   click css('.repository a').first()
 9       name "First Project Page"
10       expect status_code() == 200
11       expect css('.breadcrumb li a').text() matches '/' ~ repo_name ~ '/'
```

The set option can be used to extract data from the HTTP response (the body should be HTML, XML, or JSON). The first argument is the variable name, the second is the value. Values can be any valid expressions evaluated against the HTTP response. Here, the name of the first repository listed on the homepage is extracted into the repo_name variable. This value is then used in the next step to check the breadcrumb on the project page.

Submitting Forms

Let's submit the search form as an additional step when on the Twig page:

Listing 18-14
```
 1   endpoint 'https://gitlist.demo.blackfire.io/'
 2
```

```
3   name 'GitList Scenarios'
4
5   scenario
6       name 'Check first repository'
7
8       set query 'foo'
9
10      # steps as above
11
12      submit css('.form-search')
13          name "Search"
14          param query query
15          expect css('table.tree td').count() > 10
16          expect not (body() matches '/No results found./')
```

submit takes a button (via form("button_name")) or a form like above (as the
GitList search form does not have a button anyway). Notice that we have defined
the default value of the query variable in the set option.

Variables can also be defined or overridden via the --variable CLI flag:

Listing 18-15
```
1   blackfire-player run gitlist.bkf --variable "query=bar"
```

Crawling APIs

Crawling APIs can be done with the exact same primitives. For JSON responses,
use JSON paths in expressions:

Listing 18-16
```
1   visit url('/' ~ repo_name ~ '/network/2.x/0.json')
2       name 'Network Ajax Request'
3       expect status_code() == 200
4       expect json('repo') == repo_name
5       expect json('commitishPath') == '2.x'
```

The json() function extracts data from JSON responses by using JSON
expressions (see *JMESPath*[6] for their syntax).

Scraping Values

The css(), xpath(), and json() functions can also be used to scrape data out of
PHP responses via the set option:

Listing 18-17
```
1   visit url('/' ~ repo_name ~ '/network/2.x/0.json')
2       name 'Network Ajax Request'
3       expect status_code() == 200
4       expect json('repo') == repo_name
5       expect json('commitishPath') == '2.x'
6
```

---

6. http://jmespath.org/specification.html

```
7     # commits.keys(@) is a JMESPath expression
8     set commits json('commits.keys(@)')
```

Store a report of the execution with the extracted values via the `--json` flag:

```
Listing 18-18   1   blackfire-player run gitlist.bkf --variables "query=bar" --json > values.json
```

The `values.json` contains all variables from the scenario run:

```
Listing 18-19   1   {
               2       "name": "'GitList scenarios'",
               3       "results": [
               4           {
               5               "scenario": "'Check first repository'",
               6               "values": {
               7                   "repo_name": "Twig",
               8                   "commits": [
               9                       "1329b5580fad7a4fa9fe321973a9bb8d4631b4f3",
              10                       "43c558088e574f293f17b9e71bb67e280920748b",
              11                       "0837fda1b7b2436a4a5e104ff8241127ffeb3625",
              12                       "a14d249004b458d30024feff1a1a88806bdc5598",
              13                       "4beb7bfb0b1d120113e8ba6b82b2c4d8a902f8f4",
              14                       "70db030571b8f3b33a26f1bfc2b1e23bbbee2985",
              15                       "7a3d825969fd7f6ccaa8fb737361baa715ffb71c",
              16                       "0b819abb0dc594012577ddd2ebc91d31286ced77",
              17                       "fda20a63361c1cfa0a231025b1a24bd3900c6a97",
              18                       "03542492e99f7012ac633d09712e57ab84a565b0",
              19                       "3491e3590e6f0ff000372dabbaf9c3ba4c18ebb6",
              20                       "a0e8d58a6e7ba0edcb90cb824acdc9048de155bb",
              21                       "60a8f465d6f259c92a8fe0fb61cf8f767bd8d025",
              22                       "6a5f676b77a90823c2d4eaf76137b771adf31323",
              23                       "bcf3f82fff4da94e06b0363d26ad5d97523f65a7"
              24                   ]
              25               },
              26               "error": null
              27           }
              28       ],
              29       "message": "Build run successfully",
              30       "code": 0,
              31       "success": true,
              32       "input": {
              33           "path": "gitlist.bkf",
              34           "content": "..."
              35       }
              36   }
```

Conclusion

Blackfire Player is a very powerful Open-Source library for crawling, testing, and scraping HTTP applications. We have barely scratched the surface of all its features:

- Several scenarios can be defined in a .bkf files or in PHP;
- Abstract scenarios to reuse common steps;
- Delays between requests;
- Conditional scenarios execution based on extracted values;

- etc.

You can read Blackfire Player's extensive documentation to learn more about all its features.

Similar to Blackfire Player, there are many other Open-Source libraries that provide native integrations with Blackfire. The next chapter covers the main integrations and how you can help us adding more.

Chapter 19
Benchmarking

Web applications are not just about generating web pages or API payloads. The heart of an application is its custom business logic. The business logic is the code that is reused in all parts of a project: from generating data for mobile apps to fueling web frontends. This is also the code that should be decoupled from your framework of choice as it should survive refactoring and technology changes. Making this code fast will pay off in the long run.

An application's business logic often relies on non-trivial algorithms that can significantly affect the entire application's performance. The best way to determine which implementation of a given algorithm is faster is to use a benchmarking tool to complement Blackfire.

Blackfire can be used to understand the reasons why an algorithm is faster or slower than another one by using manual instrumentation. A benchmarking tool provides the infrastructure to run different algorithms in isolation and answer questions like which algorithm is better? Better is not always faster as using the ideal algorithm is usually a trade-off between CPU cycles and memory usage. A good benchmarking tool also provides tools for analyzing the generated statistics and guides you in analyzing the results.

In the PHP world, *PHPBench*[1] is such a tool. PHPBench goes beyond simple benchmarks as it promotes writing long-lasting benchmarks that you can keep alongside your code and your tests.

Similar to how you create a test class for your testing framework, create a bench class for your benchmarking framework:

```
class SomeBench
{
    public function benchAlgorithm()
    {
        // call the code you want to benchmark
    }
}
```

---

1. https://phpbench.readthedocs.io/

Running the bench is then a matter of using the **phpbench** utility:

Listing 19-2

```
1   phpbench run benchmarks/SomeBench.php --report=default
```

PHPBench supports many options to configure the number of iterations, data providers, before/after tasks to setup and tear down benchmarks, and more.

Chapter 20
Load-Testing

Code behavior depends on many factors, including server load. Understanding the impact of server load will prove useful when trying to optimize the performance of a codebase. Simulating load can be done via specialized Open-Source tools like *JMeter*[1] or *Gatling*[2] and by online services that can provision huge numbers of virtual machines that simulate a high number of users.

Load-testing tools work by simulating user sessions browsing your application for a period of time. These statistics can provide some insight, but they cannot explain why your code becomes slower when it is under stress. One way to get more information is to run some Blackfire scenarios (via Blackfire player) while the load is high and compare these profiles with ones generated under negligible load. The comparison graph should highlight which parts of the code degrade under stress.

Instead of using the JMeter GUI to create scenarios, use a recorder like the one provided by *Blazemeter*[3].

---

1. https://jmeter.apache.org/
2. https://gatling.io
3. https://guide.blazemeter.com/hc/en-us/articles/206732579-Chrome-Extension

Chapter 21
Profiling the Frontend

Before end-users interact with your website in a browser, they need to wait for a number of things to happen: initialization (DNS resolution, TCP connection, proxy, and SSL negotiation), server rendering, data transfer, and page rendering in the browser.

Blackfire helps you improve the performance of server rendering, but what about the other parts of the equation?

If you set aside server rendering time, most of the time a user spends waiting for a page to load is spent in the browser. There are so many things to do before the page is fully usable by the end user: first and foremost, a web page is composed of many resources besides the main contents that the browser has to resolve and load (JavaScripts and stylesheets). Then it needs to build the DOM tree from the HTML and execute any needed JavaScript. Last but not least, extensions that you installed in the browser can have an impact as well.

 Websites and many mobile applications rely on the same underlying technologies like HTTP, DNS, SSL, etc. But for mobile applications, the latency, the bandwidth, and the limited amount of resources on phones make everything more challenging. Speed matters, even on mobile — and perhaps especially on mobile.

Improving server performance is made simpler as you know everything about your infrastructure: the number of servers, their CPU, memory, bandwidth, location, and more. Client performance is much harder as users can have very different setups: location, bandwidth, computer power, internet connectivity, etc. These constraints all influence a user's experience and they are all out of your control.

This chapter is a quick overview of the tools you can use to understand and improve your application's frontend performance.

HTTP

Improving the time it takes for a webpage to be usable by a user starts with HTTP optimizations. A quick overview is given by *Google's timeline*[1]:

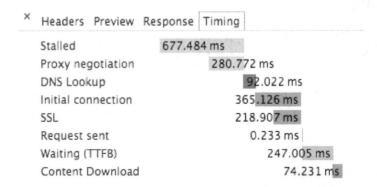

If you want to learn more about how a browser handles HTTP and possible optimizations, read *Page Weight Doesn't Matter*[2].

The Google Chrome Network tab also summarizes HTTP interactions with the user quite nicely:

 The "*High-Performance browser network*[3]" book is a great resource for an in-depth analysis of network performance.

---

1. https://developers.google.com/web/tools/chrome-devtools/profile/network-performance/resource-loading#resource-network-timing
2. https://www.speedshop.co/2015/11/05/page-weight-doesnt-matter.html
3. https://hpbn.co/

HTML and JavaScript

A browser renders a page in three basic stages: when it finishes retrieving the web contents from the server, when the interface starts to be understandable by the user (most elements are displayed), and when the user can fully interact with the page (all stylesheets and JavaScripts have been loaded and evaluated).

To get a quick overview of the browser performance of your application, use *Google PageSpeed Insights*[4]. This tool does indeed give you great insights.

The *W3C Navigation Timing*[5] recommendation allows you to "access timing information related to navigation and elements" programmatically from JavaScript.

When the Google Chrome Team introduced the RAIL model, Paul Irish started with *this great advice*[6]:

> There's no shortage of performance advice, is there? The elephant in the room is the fact that it's challenging to interpret: Everything comes with caveats and disclaimers, and sometimes one piece of advice can seem to actively contradict another. Phrases like "The DOM is slow" or "Always use CSS animations" make for great headlines, but the truth is often far more nuanced.

RAIL is a model that helps you avoid performance issues by setting general performance goals. RAIL stands for:

- **Response** (user interface): Tap to paint in less than 100ms;
- **Animation**: Layout rendering should take less than 16ms per frame;
- **Idle**: Use idle time to compute some work in chunks of 50ms;
- **Load**: The page should be fully loaded in less than 1000ms.

If you want to dive more in RAIL, watch the "Dev Tools: State of the Union" talk.

Let's see how these goals can be observed and improved.

R for Response

When a user interacts with a page by clicking a button or submitting a form, you can either load a new page or asynchronously load data to render a React component or populate an Angular scope.

---

4. https://developers.google.com/speed/pagespeed/insights
5. https://www.w3.org/TR/navigation-timing/
6. https://www.smashingmagazine.com/2015/10/rail-user-centric-model-performance/

For any interface change, 100ms is the performance goal you should target after the user triggers it from the interface. If not, you should use a loader, a progress bar, or anything that will help the user understand that the action has been taken into account.

A for Animation

Animations are exceptionally smooth for end users at 60 frames per second. That gives you 16ms per frame.

16ms is even too much according to this *article*[7]:

> Each of those frames has a budget of just over 16ms (1 second / 60 = 16.66ms). In reality, however, the browser has housekeeping work to do, so all of your work needs to be completed inside 10ms. When you fail to meet this budget the frame rate drops, and the content judders on screen. This is often referred to as **jank**, and it negatively impacts the user's experience.

You can spot janks in your pages by having a look at the "Timeline" tab of the Google Chrome developer toolbar; janks are reported with a red corner:

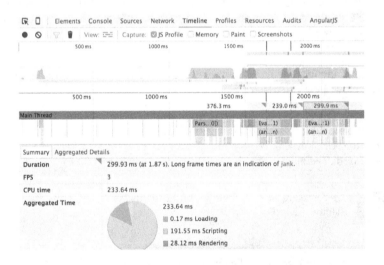

I for Idle

To avoid blocking the user interface with JavaScript, you should try to split computational tasks into small chunks and take advantage of the Page Visibility API to defer processing until when the user is idle.

Each of these chunks of idle-time work should not take more than 50ms to complete. If you have a larger task that is difficult to optimize into 50ms chunks,

---

7. https://developers.google.com/web/fundamentals/performance/rendering/

consider delegating this work to a **web-worker**. Executing JavaScript in a web-worker is like creating a new independent thread outside the page event loop. Communication with this thread happens through a messaging API. Read the *Mozilla Web Worker documentation*[8] to learn more about this technique.

 You can also read this very nice tutorial explaining how to build a *Pokemon application*[9].

Another important consideration when writing JavaScript is function calls that result in a browser flush of all pending changes. When creating DOM nodes, updating DOM node classes, or even when adding CSS properties, the requested changes are queued waiting for an upcoming refresh of the interface. Knowing which *function calls trigger an early flush*[10] can help.

L for Load

Google Chrome timeline is a great tool that you can use to record a page display process as a series of screenshots:

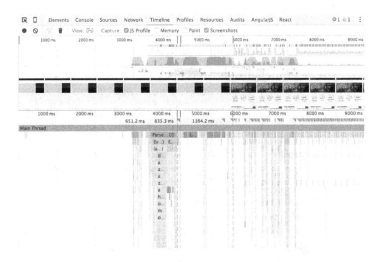

If you want to test your website from a different location than yours, or with another browser, use *webpagetest.org*[11]. This tool provides a lot of metrics to help you better understand what is happening during browsing load time and let you compare different selections of locations, browsers, etc.

---

8. https://developer.mozilla.org/en-US/docs/Web/API/Web_Workers_API/Using_web_workers
9. https://www.pocketjavascript.com/blog/2015/11/23/introducing-pokedex-org
10. https://gist.github.com/paulirish/5d52fb081b3570c81e3a
11. https://www.webpagetest.org/

Using a profiler also helps. All major browsers like Google Chrome and Firefox provide profiling tools. Trigger a JavaScript profile using the "Profile" tab of your browser developer tools.

Using Profiling Tools in your Code

The Google Chrome Profiler can be programmatically used thanks to the *console API*[12].

Inline this JavaScript snippet at the very bottom of your HTML <head> to profile all JavaScript until the window load event:

Listing 21-1
```
1  console.profile('load');
2  window.onload = function(e){
3      console.profileEnd('load');
4  }
```

For more information on how to build your own tools on top of the Chrome Remote debugging protocol, read *Pauk Irish*[13] article.

Stylesheets

Stylesheets are probably one of the most difficult parts of a website to optimize. Here is a quick overview of some optimization techniques:

- **Remove unused CSS rules**: CSS rules accumulate over time; you add new ones but rarely remove obsolete ones. Also, if you are using a CSS framework like Bootstrap or Foundation, you are probably not using more than 30% of all their features. A tool like *Uncss*[14] can help you remove unnecessary CSS rules.
- **Optimize the CSS critical path**: Inlining CSS for anything above-the-fold makes rendering faster, anything else can be loaded asynchronously; this is what a tool like *Critical*[15] does.
- **Minify and Compress your files**.
- **Analyze Stylesheets complexity**: *Parker*[16] is a tool that helps you measure CSS complexity. Complexity also comes from small things like slightly different colors used throughout your code, something that *Colorguard*[17] detects and helps resolve.

Google Chrome developer tools provide an "Audit" tab that helps diagnose some CSS issues:

---

12. https://developer.chrome.com/devtools/docs/console-api#consoleprofilelabel
13. https://github.com/paulirish/automated-chrome-profiling
14. https://github.com/giakki/uncss
15. https://github.com/addyosmani/critical
16. https://github.com/katiefenn/parker
17. https://github.com/SlexAxton/css-colorguard

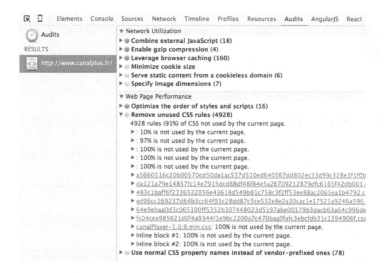

To test your optimizations, use automated tools like *PhantomCSS*[18], *huxley*[19], *Wraith*[20], or *Needle*[21].

 Also *watch*[22] Addy Osmani's *presentation*[23] on CSS performance tooling.

The Future

You should start looking at two interesting technologies that could help making your application blazing fast: Google AMP and the Service Workers API.

Google AMP for accelerated mobile pages is a project that should provide a way to write *web applications in HTML/JS using components*[24] that will be rendered fast. You can test the technology on the *project website*[25].

Service Worker API is a standard *JavaScript API*[26] that brings the power of native applications to the web. It acts as a proxy between web applications, the browser, and the network. It provides a way to handle offline usages of web applications, server push notifications, and background synchronization.

18. https://github.com/Huddle/PhantomCSS
19. https://github.com/facebookarchive/huxley
20. https://github.com/BBC-News/wraith
21. https://github.com/bfirsh/needle
22. https://www.youtube.com/watch?v=FEs2jgZBaQA
23. https://speakerdeck.com/addyosmani/css-performance-tooling
24. https://www.ampproject.org/docs/get_started/create_page.html
25. https://www.ampproject.org
26. https://developer.mozilla.org/en-US/docs/Web/API/Service_Worker_API

This blog post is an interesting read about instant loading web page using the application shell architecture and service workers.

Automating Frontend Performance

Like for unit tests, you need to keep an eye on the frontend performance in an automated way. There are quite a few tools that you can use:

- *WebPageTest*[27]: Provides a console tool to automate tests you can run on webpagetest.org;
- *Grunt Perf Budget*[28]: Enforces your performance budget, built on top of WebPageTest;
- *PageSpeedInsight*[29]: Wraps Google Page Speed Insight in a console tool;
- *Phantomas*[30]: Generates performance metrics using PhantomJS.

Conclusion

Remember that a website is only usable by your end user once the interface is understandable by the user and all blocking processes are finished.

One last piece of advice from *Addy Osmani*[31]:

> When you want to be fast, you have to give up the thing slowing you down.

27. https://github.com/marcelduran/webpagetest-api
28. https://github.com/tkadlec/grunt-perfbudget
29. https://github.com/addyosmani/psi
30. https://github.com/macbre/phantomas
31. https://www.youtube.com/watch?v=FEs2jgZBaQA

Chapter 22
Understanding PHP Internals

Understanding how PHP works goes a long way toward writing performant code. There are quite a few blogs and presentations online describing PHP internals, but very few of them are performance oriented. This chapter explains some PHP behaviors that have a direct impact on performance. This is far from being a comprehensive list of everything you need to know about how PHP works behind the scenes, but just an introduction to invite you to learn more about PHP internals.

 There's no need to understand PHP internals if you are running an old version of PHP. Getting performance improvements for free can often be achieved by upgrading to the latest PHP version.

Reference Mismatches

Reference mismatches happen anytime a **by-value** variable is passed to a **by-ref** function argument, and the other way around.

Listing 22-1
```
1  function foo($arg)
2  {
3  }
4
5  $a = "some var";
6
7  // This turns $a AND $b into references
8  $b = &$a;
9
10  // Reference mismatch
11  foo($a);
12
13  // Reference mismatch again
14  foo($b);
```

In this example, function foo() declares a by-value argument ($arg), but the foo($a) and foo($b) calls pass a reference created by line 8.

Because the function signature and the passed arguments mismatch, the PHP engine has to **duplicate the variable value in memory**, and will destroy it afterward if the function does not use the variable to send it to other function calls.

The performance impact depends on the type of the argument: duplicating an object is easy and fast, but big arrays or large strings are much slower to duplicate:

Listing 22.2

```php
1   function foo($data)
2   {
3       echo "In function: ".memory_get_usage()."\n";
4   }
5
6   echo "Initial memory: ".memory_get_usage()."\n";
7
8   $r = range(1, 1024);
9
10  // Create a reference set
11  $r2 = &$r;
12
13  echo "Array created: ".memory_get_usage()."\n";
14
15  foo($r);
16
17  echo "End of function: ".memory_get_usage()."\n";
18
19  /*
20  Initial memory:   235,664
21  Array created:    383,592
22  In function:      482,080
23  End of function: 383,624
24  */
```

The result of executing the above script is clear, passing a big array to the foo() function with a reference mismatch raises memory usage during the time of the function execution (from about 375Kb to 473Kb).

Removing the & when creating $r2 line 11 fixes the problem and memory stays stable when running the code again:

Listing 22.3

```
1   /*
2   Initial memory:   235,592
3   Array created:    383,400
4   In function:      383,432
5   End of function: 383,432
6   */
```

Using references is often used as a performance optimization, but this is not always the case. You can see in this example how creating a reference can increase memory usage significantly, and memory allocation has a direct impact on performance.

foreach Behavior

Unneeded memory increase is not always related to references. Have a look at this snippet of code:

Listing 22-4

```
1   $a = range(1, 1024);
2   $b = $a;
3   echo memory_get_usage()."\n";
4
5   foreach ($a as $v) {
6       if ($v == 1) {
7           echo memory_get_usage()."\n";
8       }
9   }
10
11  echo memory_get_usage()."\n" ;
12
13  /*
14  373,936
15  472,512
16  374,056
17  */
```

No references around, but the **foreach()** loop consumes a significant amount of memory. Calling **$b = $a** is very fast as PHP uses copy-on-write (its **refcount** is incremented). But when **foreach()** receives **$a**, and because it accepts a by-value variable, it has to duplicate the value because it does not know if you are going to modify the iterated value inside the loop.

If the **refcount** was one, then no duplication would have to happen in the **foreach** loop and memory would not increase.

Now, have a look at the following snippet and try to guess if memory is going to increase within the **foreach** loop:

Listing 22-5

```
1   $a = range(1, 1024);
2
3   // Create a reference set
4   $b = &$a;
5   echo memory_get_usage()."\n";
6
7   foreach ($a as $v) {
8       if ($v == 1) {
9           echo memory_get_usage()."\n";
10      }
11  }
12
13  echo memory_get_usage()."\n";
```

If you think memory increases because of the reference set, you are wrong. Here are the numbers when running the code:

Listing 22-6

```
1   /*
2   373,936
3   374,056
4   374,056
5   */
```

PHP does not have to duplicate the variable because the content is the same for all references; the refcount does not even matter.

This example demonstrates how guessing PHP behavior can be quite hard without understanding how it works. Learning more about PHP references is a good place to start your lessons.

__invoke() and Dynamic Function Calls

A dynamic call occurs when the function name is stored in a variable:

Listing 22-7
```
1  $a = 'foo';
2
3  $a();
```

Most PHP developers know that this is bad for performance. For regular function calls, PHP computes a string hash **at compilation**, which is then used to lookup the function at runtime. But for dynamic calls, PHP is forced to make the same computation **at runtime**. Moreover, functions being case insensitive, the engine is also forced to strtolower() the function name each time you call it.

A few calls do not make a difference, but many calls in a recursive function or in a loop can have a significant performance impact.

Even for regular function calls, PHP might not optimize the call:

Listing 22-8
```
1  foo();
2
3  function foo()
4  {
5  }
```

Defining a function after using it is perfectly valid, but when the compiler deals with the foo() function call, it knows nothing about the foo() definition as it is not declared yet, so it generates OPCodes that force the runtime engine to resolve the function call (look it up in a hashtable), something that can be prevented by moving the function definition above the function call.

Note that **OPcache automatically optimizes this case for you**.

Implementation Details matter

On the same topic, calling __invoke() on a closure is slower than letting PHP handle it itself:

```
Listing 22.9   1  $a = function () {
               2  };
               3
               4  $a->__invoke();
```

This is because __invoke() does not exist in the **Closure** class, it is emulated by reflection. This emulation forces the PHP engine to build the internal function call and pass it to the executor. Calling $a() does not have this overhead.

A simple benchmark will show that calling __invoke() on a closure is about twice as slow as a direct invocation.

Realpath Cache Size

Every time a PHP script tries to access a file, a directory, or a link, the operating system must resolve its realpath via the lstat() system call. This call is fast, but it involves a context switch with the kernel.

PHP will cache up to 16k of realpath accesses by default, but this cache size is too small for PHP applications that are composed of thousands of files and directories. You can increase the cache size by setting the realpath_cache_size ini setting in php.ini.

But instead of guessing the best value, configure a high value first (1Mb), use realpath_cache_size() at the end of your application to see how much cache is used by your application, and adjust the php.ini value accordingly.

PHP 7 Packed Arrays

PHP 7 has been rewritten with performance in mind. A lot of work has been done to reduce memory allocations and memory usage. One such example is the new PHP 7 "packed array."

When using contiguous integer keys, PHP7 packs the array in memory, to make it consume less:

```
Listing 22-10  1  $m = memory_get_usage();
               2
               3  // Create a packed array of keys from 1 to 1024
               4  $a = range(1, 1024);
               5
               6  echo memory_get_usage() - $m;
```

PHP 5.6 shows a memory usage of about 280Kb for this script, but under PHP 7, memory usage is about 30Kb, which is roughly ten times less (OPcache optimizes it even more).

When keys are not integers or contiguous, memory usage rises significantly:

Listing 22-11

```
1  $m = memory_get_usage();
2
3  // Create a packed array of keys from 1 to 1024
4  $a = range(1, 1024);
5
6  // Break the packed array
7  $a['a'] = 8;
8
9  echo memory_get_usage() - $m;
```

On the example above, the array in PHP 7 now uses about 70Kb of memory, which is more than double what the packed array uses.

Conclusion

As demonstrated in this chapter, knowing how PHP works under the hood helps understand PHP code performance. Don't draw conclusions too fast though; measure first.

Chapter 23
Continuous Integration

Continuously deploying code is the holy grail for any project. It starts with having confidence that changes to be deployed do not contain regressions in terms of features and performance.

The best way to avoid performance regressions is to integrate Blackfire into your continuous integration workflow. This chapter describes how you can achieve that.

Triggering Blackfire Scenarios

The easiest way to integrate Blackfire into your continuous integration and deployment workflow is to run the Blackfire scenarios you have defined in **.blackfire.yml** each time you deploy your code to testing, staging, and production. Blackfire will run tests on your pre-defined key HTTP endpoints and the build result will turn red if you are over-budget.

Whatever the tool you are using, you can automate the trigger thanks to the webhook as seen in a previous chapter:

Listing 23-1

```
1  curl -X POST https://blackfire.io/api/v1/build/env/ENV-UUID/webhook \
2      --user "$user_id:$user_token" \
3      -d "endpoint=http://symfony.com/" \
4      -d "title=Deploy v1.0.0"
```

If you are using Git tags to deploy on various environments, you can parametrize the title with the right tag name thanks to this small shell script:

Listing 23-2

```
1  LAST_TAG=`git for-each-ref --format='%(*committerdate:raw)%(committerdate:raw)
2  %(refname:short)' refs/tags | sort -n -r | awk '{ print $3; }' | head -n 1`
3
4  curl -X POST https://blackfire.io/api/v1/build/env/ENV-UUID/webhook \
5      --user "$user_id:$user_token" \
6      -d "endpoint=http://symfony.com/" \
7      -d "title=Deploy $LAST_TAG"
```

In addition to checking for performance regressions, you can also check the performance evolution between two deployments. Blackfire allows such tests via assertions if you use the `diff()` or `percent()` functions.

The webhook does not run comparison tests unless you trigger them explicitly by providing two additional parameters: `external_id`, the reference for the current build and `external_parent_id`, the reference for the previous related build. The values of these settings are free-form but they need to be unique identifiers for builds they refer to. If you are using Git, it is recommended to use the sha1s of the related tag commits.

When Blackfire receives a payload containing an `external_parent_id` setting, it looks for a previous build that matches the value and runs the comparison tests between the current profiles and the ones in the build it just found.

With the help of some simple shell commands, you can create a generic webhook that works for any deploy:

Listing 23-3

```
1  LAST_TAG=`git for-each-ref --format='%(*committerdate:raw)%(committerdate:raw)
2  %(refname:short)' refs/tags | sort -n -r | awk '{ print $3; }' | head -n 1`
3  LAST_TAG_COMMIT=`git for-each-ref
4  --format='%(*committerdate:raw) %(refname:short)
5  %(*objectname) %(objectname)' refs/tags | sort -n -r | awk '{ print $4; }' | head
6  -n 1`
7  PREVIOUS_TAG_COMMIT=`git for-each-ref
8  --format='%(*committerdate:raw)%(committerdate:raw) %(refname:short)
9  %(*objectname) %(objectname)' refs/tags | sort -n -r | awk '{ print $4; }' | head
10 -n 2 | sed '1,1d'`

curl -X POST https://blackfire.io/api/v1/build/env/ENV-UUID/webhook \
    --user "$user_id:$user_token" \
    -d "endpoint=http://symfony.com/" \
    -d "title=Deploy $LAST_TAG" \
    -d "external_id=$LAST_TAG_COMMIT" \
    -d "external_parent_id=$PREVIOUS_TAG_COMMIT"
```

 This technique works for integration tools like Jenkins or Travis, and for deployment tools like Capistrano, Chef, Puppet, or Ansible.

Using the PHP SDK and Running Unit Tests

You can do the same configuration when creating a build with the PHP SDK:

Listing 23-4

```
1  $build = $blackfire->startBuild('env_name_or_uuid', array(
2      'title' => 'Deploy '.$LAST_TAG,
3  ));
4
5  $scenario = $blackfire->startScenario($build, array(
6      'external_id' => $LAST_TAG_COMMIT,
7      'external_parent_id' => $PREVIOUS_TAG_COMMIT,
8  ));
```

Having this support in the PHP SDK means that you can configure your Blackfire unit tests to benefit from comparison tests.

This is a unique feature: for the first time, tests can **check the evolution of key metrics between two runs**. This is something you cannot do with traditional test libraries.

 The Guzzle integration benefits from the same feature as it uses the PHP SDK.

Using the Player

Going one step further, you can use Blackfire Player to run complex scenarios for your website or API whenever you deploy. Setting the external id and the external parent id is possible via environment variables:

```
1  BLACKFIRE_EXTERNAL_ID=$LAST_TAG_COMMIT \
2  BLACKFIRE_EXTERNAL_PARENT_ID=$PREVIOUS_TAG_COMMIT \
3  blackfire-player run tests.bkf -vvv --blackfire-env=ENV-UUID
```

Testing Pull Requests

We have seen how to use Git tags to configure the Blackfire webhook and unlock comparison tests between deploys. This technique can also be used to compare two arbitrary sha1s. This is exactly what you need in order to test a GitHub pull request.

If you are a GitHub user, Blackfire can automatically change the status of your pull requests. You need to configure the GitHub notification channel for your Blackfire environment:

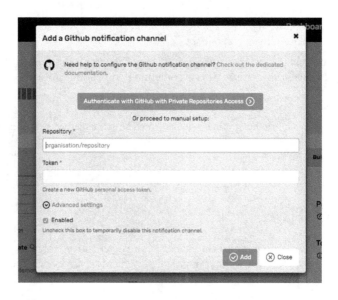

Enter the **Repository** name (like **FriendsOfPhp/Sami**) and a valid **Token** that you can generate from *GitHub*[1].

Then, whenever you want to associate a build with a pull request, set the **external_id** to the sha1 of the last commit of the pull request. From there, everything is automated and Blackfire will send the build result as a commit status associated with the pull request:

If you are a *Platform.sh*[2] user, follow our *Platform.sh instructions*[3] to tightly integrate Platform.sh auto-deployment of pull requests, automatic Blackfire scenarios triggers, and GitHub statuses on pull requests.

If you are a *Magento Commerce Cloud*[4] user, follow our *Magento Commerce Cloud instructions*[5] to tightly integrate Magento Cloud auto-deployment of pull requests, automatic Blackfire scenarios triggers, and GitHub statuses on pull requests.

---

1. https://github.com/settings/tokens/new
2. https://accounts.platform.sh/platform/trial/symfony/setup
3. https://blackfire.io/docs/integrations/platformsh
4. https://devdocs.magento.com/guides/v2.2/cloud/bk-cloud.html

Conclusion

Blackfire is not a standalone tool. It integrates seamlessly with the tools you are already using on a day-to-day basis. Continuous performance management can be a click of the mouse away.

---

5. https://devdocs.magento.com/guides/v2.2/cloud/project/project-integrate-blackfire.html

Chapter 24
Another Look at Blackfire

Blackfire is the only product on the market that provides an end-to-end performance management solution that helps companies supervise application performance throughout the product lifecycle.

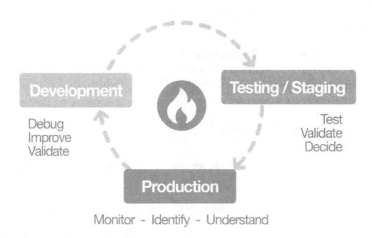

Let's quickly review Blackfire's role at each of these stages.

Using Blackfire during Development

During development, developers can use Blackfire as a super-charged profiler on their local machines to:

- Debug identified performance problems (coming from monitoring alerts in production for instance);
- Measure and improve performance by spotting performance bottlenecks;

- Write tests to set a performance budget and avoid regressions (both unit tests and scenarios);
- Validate code changes when adding new features and fixing bugs by comparing profiles;
- Understand code behavior of unknown codebases at runtime;
- Fix quality or security issues discovered via Blackfire's recommendations.

Using Blackfire on Testing Servers

On integration servers, Blackfire helps automate performance management by:

- Running tests to continuously check code behavior and performance sensitive functions;
- Running integration scenarios to find regressions and check the performance budget.

Using Blackfire on Staging Servers

If you have access to a staging environment that replicates the production one, Blackfire can be used to:

- Validate performance improvements;
- Run integration tests with production-like data;
- Decide when code is ready to be deployed to production.

Using Blackfire on Production Servers

On production servers, Blackfire is complementary to the monitoring system you already have in place. It allows you to:

- Identify the root causes of performance issues;
- Understand how your code behaves under stress;
- Find security issues even if no code changed (new vulnerabilities discovered in PHP for instance).

Conclusion

Blackfire is a unique SaaS-delivered Performance Management Solution; it allows your development and DevOps teams to measure, compare, and improve performance at every step of the application development lifecycle.

We are always looking for great stories about how Blackfire has helped our users find bottlenecks and improve the performance of their apps. Feel free to Contact us if you are interested in sharing your experience with Blackfire.

Happy profiling!

CPSIA information can be obtained
at www.ICGtesting.com
Printed in the USA
BVHW092355080719
552899BV00002B/2/P

9 782918 390367